Booktalking Around the World

Booktalking Around the World

Great Global Reads for Ages 9-14

Sonja Cole

LIBRARIES UNLIMITED

AN IMPRINT OF ABC-CLIO, LLC
Santa Barbara, California • Denver, Colorado • Oxford, England

Library of Congress Cataloging-in-Publication Data

Cole, Sonja.
　　Booktalking around the world : great global reads for ages 9-14 / Sonja Cole.
　　p. cm.
　Includes bibliographical references and index.
　ISBN 978-1-59884-613-3 (pbk. : acid-free paper) — ISBN 978-1-59884-614-0 (ebook) 1. Book talks—United States. 2. Geography—Juvenile literature—Bibliography. 3. World history—Juvenile literature—Bibliography. 4. Ethnology—Juvenile literature—Bibliography. 5. Children's literature, American—Bibliography. 6. Children's literature—21st century—Bibliography. I. Title.
Z1003.15C696 2010
021.7—dc22　　　2010036580

ISBN: 978-1-59884-613-3
EISBN: 978-1-59884-614-0

14 13 12 11 10　1 2 3 4 5

This book is also available on the World Wide Web as an eBook.
Visit www.abc-clio.com for details.

Libraries Unlimited
An Imprint of ABC-CLIO, LLC

ABC-CLIO, LLC
130 Cremona Drive, P.O. Box 1911
Santa Barbara, California 93116-1911

This book is printed on acid-free paper ∞"
Manufactured in the United States of America

Contents

Introduction

Why Booktalk Around the World?

Wouldn't it be great to have kids clamoring to learn more about ancient Egypt or the war in Iraq? Wouldn't you love to know that your students were excited to go home and learn more about the part of the world you are covering in your class? Using literature to supplement your lessons can transport kids right into the theme you are teaching. Reading fiction and narrative nonfiction, kids become immersed in the setting and make discoveries far beyond the facts they glean from their textbooks. Most important, though, reading great books inspires them to investigate further. It makes them want to know more because, having become immersed in the book they are reading, they become invested in knowing more. Wouldn't your job be so much easier if your students were already invested in learning about your subject?

Great literature can help you do that, and great booktalks can help you get that message to your students. Librarians and reading and language arts teachers know the power of booktalking to make kids excited about a book. As a school librarian, I often field teachers' requests for book lists about a particular subject to give to their students as extra credit, as a lesson extension, or to help with research assignments. Book lists are a great resource for students who are already motivated to read, but reluctant readers are likely to toss a book list in the trash, if they touch it at all. How can you grab these students and make them excited about reading? Booktalk!

A booktalk is a short summary of a book's conflict and a taste of its plotline. The point is to give just enough detail about the book so students will want to read the rest, but not so much detail that you give it all away. An engaging booktalk can stimulate students' prior knowledge, encourage them to actively predict what will happen in the book, and intrinsically motivate them to find out whether their predictions are correct. What skills or equipment do you need to booktalk? None whatsoever. You are used to selling your lesson every day; a booktalk is just an extension of that. It's a new sales trick to hook your kids into your content area.

Booktalking Around the World can be used to introduce a country unit, extend learning, facilitate further research, or stimulate interest in different countries. A social studies teacher can extend a unit on ancient Greece by booktalking a few titles that students can check out for extra credit. A Spanish teacher can generate excitement about Spanish culture by booktalking a group of titles from Spanish-speaking countries. The beauty of the booktalk in the classroom is its versatility. You can spend an entire class period booktalking, or you can do a quick three-minute booktalk at the beginning or end of a period or in the middle of a lesson to segue into the next activity. Once you get the hang of it, you can teach kids to booktalk, and they can share their excitement with the rest of the class until you have a whole class full of students reading books, and talking and getting excited about them as well.

This book will arm you with ready-to-go booktalks for fiction and nonfiction books set in every continent around the globe. Where there are video booktalks available on the Internet, links are included. Each section also includes a list of related titles to encourage further reading. My hope is that you will use the booktalks in this book, see the ways literature can inject excitement into your units, and then go out on your own to find more books and give your own booktalks to kids.

How Did I Choose These Books?

I chose books that are actually set in the country of interest. Thus, books about immigration to the United States were generally not included unless a significant portion of the book takes place in the country of origin. There are a few exceptions to this rule, but for the most part, I tried to be consistent. If a book takes place in more than one country, I included it in both country chapters.

I looked at awards lists from 2000 through 2009 and included Newbery winners, Pura Belpré winners, Jane Addams Award winners, Notable Social Studies and Science Trade books, ALA Notable books, starred reviews, and some of my own personal favorites that haven't won awards but that I think should have. I wasn't absolutely strict about excluding books I love from the 1990s, so you will find a few of those here as well.

For each country, I tried to balance the ratio of nonfiction and fiction. I also tried to balance the ratio of boy characters and girl characters. I hope there is something for every reader here.

The booktalks are mostly all chapter books, although I did include several picture books for older readers in the book lists. All of the books are appropriate for Grades 3 through 8 unless I indicated "Grades 7 and up." These are what I call "Rated PG-13." They contain somewhat more adult themes that younger children might not be ready for.

How the Booktalks Are Organized

I've arranged these booktalks within eight major categories—Africa; Asia; Europe; South and Central America; North America; Australia, New Zealand, and the South Pacific Islands; the Arctic and Antarctica; and Ancient Civilizations. Within these chapters, further subdivisions focus on specific countries, such as China, Russia, and England. In the case of some continents, such as Africa, there were not enough titles for any specific country to warrant a separate subdivision, so the country names are stated in the bibliographic line.

For each booktalk, you'll find bibliographic information and interest levels and reading levels (when available), along with complete booktalks, ready to use as they are or to adapt to fit your own booktalking style. IL refers to the interest level of the book, so a book that says **IL** 4–8 would be interesting and developmentally appropriate for a child in fourth through eighth grades. RL refers to the reading level based on grade norms, so a book that says **RL** 3.3 matches the average reading ability of a child in the third month of third grade. Award-winning titles are noted with a ♈ symbol. You'll also find book lists with brief annotations that you can use as quick one-sentence booktalks or develop into your own longer booktalks.

Quick Tips for Booktalk Presentations

1. *Be passionate.* The right book can change a child's life, and your booktalk might be the first introduction to this life-changing book. That's a big deal! Own it. Open up and let the magic happen!

2. *Be sincere.* You don't have to love the book, but you should be able to honestly and earnestly tell kids why they might love it. Not every book is a good candidate for a booktalk. If I can't find any reason to recommend a book sincerely, I don't booktalk it.

3. *Be authentic.* I wrote these booktalks the way I talk to kids. If you need to change them to make them sound more like you, then please do. Using your own voice in a booktalk is a way to "keep it real," and that's a powerful way to connect with kids.

Booktalking FAQs

I'm nervous about doing a booktalk. How do I get started?

I was nervous too, so I totally understand. Don't feel like you have to dive in the deep end right away. Get your feet wet in small ways. Build up your confidence until booktalking is second nature. Do informal one-on-one booktalks with your most receptive kids or with other teachers. Gather your star readers for a practice booktalk during lunch or after school. (They might want to give their own booktalks, too. Now you have an extracurricular booktalking club and support group!) Start the day with one booktalk before you get into the lesson. If it bombs, you just regroup and get on with your day. When you are passionate, sincere, and authentic in your booktalk, kids will respond in equally passionate, sincere, and authentic ways. Yeah, that's a little scary sometimes, but it can also be thrilling and delightful.

I can't possibly read all these books! Do I have to read every book that I booktalk?

No, but I always admit when I haven't read the entire book. This is important to maintain your credibility with the kids. If I haven't read the book, I will invite kids to read it and give me their opinion. It's fun when they can recommend books to adults, too. That said, it is much easier to be passionate about a book that you have actually read and loved, so I do recommend that you try to read as many books as you can.

How do I keep kids actively engaged during a booktalk presentation?

I ask kids to keep a list of all the titles I talk about and to rate them. You can do this in a couple of ways. You can hand out a list of titles you know you are going to be booktalking. Or if booktalking is an ongoing part of your curriculum, you can ask kids to keep a reading journal where they write down and rate all the books you booktalk throughout the year. That way, whenever they need a new book to read, they can just look in their journals and pick one.

Should you show the book while you're booktalking?

I do. It gives kids something to look at. It activates their prior knowledge and gives context to what they are hearing about the book. Sometimes kids want to hold the book and look through it while I'm booktalking. This I do not allow. It is distracting to them and to me. But I always make sure to leave some extra time after the booktalk for kids to look more closely at all the books.

What if every kid wants to read the same book, and there is only one copy?

You must have given a knockout booktalk! Well done, you! What I do in this happy situation is start a reserve list. Kids sign up for the books they want, and everyone gets their turn. If your administration allows, set aside a petty cash fund, so you can run to the bookstore and buy emergency copies of super-popular books. On days when I'm going to be booktalking for several groups of kids, I do different books for every group. Rotating through a bunch of titles helps ensure that everyone gets to go home with a book they are excited about.

Thank you for working to make kids excited about books. I truly believe that a love of reading will change their lives, and therefore make the world a better place!

Chapter 1

Africa

With the discovery of the ancient hominid "Lucy," scientists believe that Africa is the birthplace of human life 200,000 years ago. Reading the books listed in this chapter, it is impossible not to notice the physical grandeur of this huge continent, a continent so big that the United States could fit in it three times! It is also impossible not to notice the devastating impact that colonialism has had on Africa. It is still suffering from the effects caused by prejudice, war, corruption, and the upheaval of native traditions and life. But there are stories of amazing people like Nelson Mandela and Wangari Maathai who have changed the lives of Africans and inspired the whole world. From interracial friendship to interspecies friendship (see *Owen & Mzee*), these books will inspire kids to learn more about Africa.

Africa Booktalks

Fiction

Colfer, Eoin. *Benny and Omar* (Hyperion, 2007) 288p. Tunisia. IL 5–9 RL 3.3
Benny lives in Ireland with his family, and he is obsessed with hurling, a sport similar to hockey. When his father announces that he is being transferred to Tunisia in northern Africa for work, Benny is pretty mad. Then when he gets there, his sarcastic attitude does not make him any

friends at the international school where he goes with other kids from all over the world. The first real friend he makes in Africa is a local orphan boy named Omar. Omar lives on the streets. The only English he knows is what he learned by watching American TV shows—his word for "hospital" is "Chicago Hope" and his word for "brother" is "Bee Gees." Their attempts at communicating are hilarious. At the beginning of the book, Benny is kind of a jerk, but his friendship with Omar changes him; by the end, readers will be rooting for both of them.

Marsden, Carolyn, and Philip Matzigkeit. *Sahwira: An African Friendship* (Candlewick, 2009) 189p. **Zimbabwe.** **IL** 5–8 **RL** 3.5

In the 1960s, the country in southern Africa now known as Zimbabwe was a British colony called Rhodesia. During that time, the native Africans wanted independence, and tensions between white settlers and natives were high. But Evan, a white American boy living with his missionary parents, is inspired by the news he hears of Martin Luther King Jr., and he feels torn between two worlds. At the Christian mission where he lives, his best friend is a native boy named Blessing, but at the whites-only school in town, his classmates and teachers expect him to train to fight natives in the impending war of independence. Evan doesn't know what to do. Blessing's native friends are pressuring him, too. As the story goes on, their friendship seems more and more impossible. Can blacks and whites really be equal in an African country on the brink of a war?

Mead, Alice. *Year of No Rain* (FSG, 2003) 129p. **Sudan.** **IL** 5–8 **RL** 4.9

Eleven-year-old Stephen lives with his mother and sister in Sudan. It is 1999, and it hasn't rained for over two years, so survival is difficult, but so far they have managed. They still have two cows and can get milk from them so they won't starve or die of thirst. Still Stephen thinks it's great when a humanitarian group drops food for the village. But it turns out to be the worst thing that could ever happen. The Civil War has mostly stayed away from their village, but when the soldiers hear about the food, they raid the village and burn it to the ground. Stephen and his two friends escaped, but now have no shelter, no food, and, worst of all, no water. They've heard of refugee camps for people like them, but they are hundreds of miles away. How can they walk all that way with no food, no water, and no protection from the wild animals or soldiers they meet along the way?

Naidoo, Beverley. *Burn My Heart* (Amistad, 2007) 207p. **Kenya.** **IL** 5–9 **RL** 4

In Kenya in the 1950s, white settlers were the landowners, and the native Kenyans were the workers on the land that their ancestors used to own before the Europeans came to Africa. That's the situation of Mugo, a Kikuyu boy living and working on his family's ancestral land that has been settled by a white British family. He sometimes hangs out with the owner's son, Mathew, but he always has to remember his place as a servant in the kitchen. One day, Mathew makes a terrible mistake that sets off a chain of events with disastrous consequences for Mugo and his family. This story is fictional, but it's based on this time in history when some of the native Kikuyu tribe got angry and rose up against the white landowners. Now Kenya is a democratic country where everyone has a vote, both native Africans and whites, but this book describes a time when both groups were afraid and mistrustful of the other.

Park, Linda Sue. *A Long Walk to Water: Based on a True Story* (Clarion, 2010) 120p. **Sudan.** **IL** 5–8 **RL** 6

Imagine being in school one day when all of a sudden you hear gunshots outside. Your teacher tells you to run away from the school, but no matter what, don't go home. That's what happens to Salva when the war in Sudan comes to his village. Salva runs away into the African wilderness and tries to find a safe place to hide. He never goes home but ends up traveling for years from one refugee camp to another. Meanwhile, a girl named Nya has to walk for miles every day back and forth to get water for her family. She can't go to school or play with her friends because her most important job every day is to get water. Without it, she and her family will die. By the end of this book, Nya and Salva meet, and you find out how their true story ends.

Video Booktalk: http://bookwink.com/archive_2010_10_01.html

Scaletta, Kurtis. *Mamba Point* (Knopf, 2010) 271p. **Liberia.** **IL** 4–7 **RL** 4.2

Twelve-year-old Linus has never been the bravest kid, so after he finds out that his father is being transferred from Ohio to a new job in the U.S. Embassy in Liberia, he has a panic attack in school. Linus decides to make a fresh start in Liberia and not be such a 'fraidy-cat. His new home in Liberia is full of real danger, though, including the deadly black mamba snake, which can move faster than a human and whose venom takes about fifteen minutes to kill you if you don't get the antidote in time. It's pretty much the world's deadliest snake. His parents assure him that mambas are rare, but he keeps seeing them wherever he goes. It's like they are following him. Then Linus learns about the African belief in animal spirits, or *kasengs*. When you have a *kaseng,* it's believed that you are connected with the animal, and it will protect you. Linus is starting to think he might have this *kaseng* thing with the mamba, so he tests it. The next time he sees the snake, he tries being Brave Linus, and he lets the snake get close enough to touch him, eventually even hiding the snake in his room! You can understand what a terrible idea this is, right? If the snake gets loose in the house, it could kill someone. The new Linus is not worried, but maybe he should be . . .

Whelan, Gloria. *Listening for Lions* (HarperCollins, 2005) 208p. **Kenya. IL** 4–8 **RL** 6.5

The year is 1919, and thirteen-year-old Rachel lives in British East Africa with her missionary parents. She was born there and loves everything about Africa, the wild animals, the stories of the native Kikuyu tribe, even working at the mission hospital. She and her parents are happy in Africa, and they never want to go back to England. But when the deadly influenza epidemic hits their village, both of Rachel's parents die, and she is completely alone. The Pritchards, a British family that lives nearby, take her in and treat her like a daughter, which is strange because they had a daughter who also died in the epidemic. She had red hair like Rachel, and now they are telling people that it was Rachel who died and that their daughter Valerie is still alive. It turns out the Pritchards are using Rachel in a greedy scheme. They want her to go to England, pretending to be Valerie, and convince Valerie's rich grandfather to give them more money. The grandfather is angry at the Pritchards, but he's never met Valerie, so they think Rachel will fool him and charm him into being more generous. Rachel doesn't want to do this for several reasons: She doesn't want to leave Africa, she doesn't want to lie, and she doesn't want to help the Pritchards, who are horrible people. But she knows her only alternative is to go to an orphanage and even face worse treatment, so what can she do? Read this book to find out.

Yohalem, Eve. *Escape Under the Forever Sky* (Chronicle, 2009) 220p. **Ethiopia. IL** 5–8 **RL** 5.4

Thirteen-year-old Lucy is the daughter of the American ambassador in Ethiopia. She wants to be a conservation zoologist when she grows up, so she thought she would love being in Africa. But her mother doesn't let her go exploring because she thinks it's too dangerous. So Lucy spends all her time either at school or at home reading about the animals she wishes she could go outside and see for herself. Her overprotective mother won't even let her go out with her friends in the city because she is afraid something will happen. So of course, Lucy sneaks out. And guess what? Something bad happens! Up until this point, the book is pretty predictable, but then Lucy gets kidnapped, and the story really gets good. After a few days, she realizes that no one is going to come rescue her, and she will have to escape on her own. But how? And will she be able to survive in the bush with no food or water, and animals that would be happy to rip out her throat? This book is actually based on the true story of a girl who was kidnapped in Ethiopia in 2005 and was rescued by lions.

Nonfiction

Goodall, Jane. *The Chimpanzees I Love: Saving Their World and Ours* (Scholastic, 2001) 80p. **Tanzania.** **IL** 4–9 **RL** 5.9

As a child, Jane Goodall always wanted to study animals. This book describes how she made that dream come true and became famous for studying chimpanzees in Tanzania. Chimpanzees are more like humans than any other creature living today, yet Dr. Goodall was the first to discover much of what we know about chimps. By watching them constantly, she figured out that chimpanzees in the wild act a lot like humans. They are very social; they hold hands with and kiss their friends. But they make war with outside chimps, ganging up on and even killing them. The males have contests of strength and aggression to determine the leader of the pack. They even know how to make a tool for digging termites out of the dirt so they can eat them. That's pretty sophisticated! No other animals except humans make tools. Although chimps don't have vocal cords that allow them to speak our language, they can be taught sign language and communicate with people that way. They even invent new signs for words they don't know—like "listen drink" for soda. Ingenious! The chimps express emotions and take care of each other in such sweet ways. The adorable pictures will have you saying "Aww," on every page.

Hatkoff, Craig, Isabella Hatkoff, and Paula Kuhumbu. *Owen & Mzee: The True Story of a Remarkable Friendship.* Photog. Peter Greste (Scholastic, 2006) 32p. **Kenya.** **IL** K–5 **RL** 4.7

Hippopotami and giant tortoises don't normally become friends. In fact, they could really hurt each other if they wanted to, but in this true story, you find out how a baby hippo named Owen becomes best friends with a 130-year-old tortoise named Mzee (pronounced mm-ZAY). It all started on December 26, 2004, when an earthquake sent a huge tsunami all across the Indian Ocean, destroying coastal villages and killing lots of people. Owen was with his mother and a group of other hippopotami on the coast of Kenya when the wave hit. When rescuers got there, only little baby Owen was left, stranded and alone without his mother to take care of him. The rescuers sent him to an animal sanctuary where he could be free but still taken care of by the workers there. As soon as he arrived, he went straight to the old tortoise Mzee and just snuggled down next to him like he was his mother! At first Mzee didn't like being followed around by a hippo, but now the two are inseparable. If you like really adorable true animal stories, you will love *Owen & Mzee*. See also *Looking for Miza: The True Story of the Mountain Gorilla Family Who Rescued One of Their Own* (Scholastic, 2008).

🏆 Nivola, Claire A. *Planting the Trees of Kenya: The Story of Wengari Maathai* (FSG, 2008) 32p. **Kenya.** 🟦 K–5 🟥 7.4. Jane Addams Award

How can planting trees change an entire country? In science class, you might have learned how destructive soil erosion is. When there is nothing to hold the soil in place, the wind can blow it all around. It can end up in your water so you can't drink it, and there will be no topsoil where crops can grow. This is what happened in Kenya, and it was really ruining the people's lives until a brave woman named Wangari Maathai started a program to plant trees all across the country. Because of her, the people of Kenya were able to save their environment, have clean water to drink, and protect their crops so they had food to eat and sell. Wangari's program changed their lives so much that she won the Nobel Peace Prize.

Reef, Catherine. *This Our Dark Country: The American Settlers of Liberia* (Clarion, 2002) 136p. **Liberia.** 🟦 6–9 🟥 8

Did you know that when the slave trade ended, there was a group of white Americans who wanted to send the slaves back to Africa? This book describes how in 1822, the West African country of Liberia became an American colony for free blacks and former slaves. They named the colony Liberia for liberty, but even though they were free in Liberia, life was extremely difficult. They had to clear the land and build everything from the ground up. They depended on shipments of food from the United States, and they also depended on U.S. military support when they were attacked by the African warriors whose land the settlers had stolen. Hunger and war were bad enough but the biggest cause of death for the settlers was malaria; they had no idea how to prevent it or treat it. Over time, they managed to create an American-style civilization with schools and Christian churches. But sadly, even though the American-Liberians were all originally from Africa, they considered themselves superior to the native Africans and did not give them equal rights in the new colony. Now almost two hundred years later, this country that started with the goal of liberty and freedom for blacks faces poverty and violent turmoil because they have never been able to live in peace and equality.

Africa Book List

The glory of this continent's landscape, animals, and the inspiring fictional and true stories of brave people who overcame prejudice, hatred, and ignorance are all here in the books that follow.

Fiction

Doder, Joshua. *Grk: Operation Tortoise* (Delacorte, 2007) 219p. **Seychelles.** **IL** 4–7 **RL** 3.4

While vacationing in the Seychelles, Tim uncovers a devious plot that threatens the endangered local tortoise. Can he and his brave and intelligent dog Grk thwart the plot and get home alive? See also the other books in the Grk series.

Doherty, Berlie. *The Girl Who Saw Lions* (Roaring Brook, 2007) 249p. **Tanzania.** **IL** 5–7 **RL** 4.5

When both Abela's parents in Tanzania die of AIDS, Abela is forced to endure horrible treatment until she is adopted by a family in England.

♥ Ellis, Deborah. *The Heaven Shop* (Fitzhenry and Whiteside, 2004) 186p. **Malawi.** **IL** 5–9 **RL** 5.6. Jane Addams Honor

Inspired by a true story, this book tells what life is like for a thirteen-year-old AIDS orphan in Malawi.

Kessler, Cristina. *The Best Beekeeper in Lalibela: A Tale from Africa.* Illus. Leonard Jenkins (Holiday House, 2006) 32p. **Ethiopia.** **IL** 1–4 **RL** 5

In this picture book, an Ethiopian girl is determined to be a beekeeper even though it is traditionally a man's job.

Naidoo, Beverley. *The Other Side of Truth* (HarperCollins, 2001) 272p. **Nigeria.** **IL** 5–8 **RL** 5.5

Twelve-year-old Sade's father is a journalist who dares to criticize the corrupt government in Nigeria. When Sade's mother is murdered, her father arranges for Sade and her younger brother to be smuggled to their uncle in London for safety.

🏆 **Naidoo, Beverley.** *Out of Bounds: Seven Stories of Conflict and Hope* (HarperCollins, 2001) 175p. **South Africa.** 🔲 5–8 🔲 5.3. Jane Addams Award

> Seven stories chronicle a different decade in South Africa's history of apartheid and recent democracy.

Smith, Roland. *Cryptid Hunters* (Hyperion, 2005) 348p. **Congo.** 🔲 5–8 🔲 4.9

> A cryptid is an animal whose existence has not yet been proven scientifically. When Grace and Marty's uncle goes to the Congolese jungle in search of a dinosaur and its clutch of eggs, the two kids join the adventure. See also the sequel *Tentacles* (Scholastic, 2009).

St. John, Lauren. *The White Giraffe* (Dial, 2007) 192p. **South Africa.** 🔲 4–7 🔲 6

> When Martine's parents are killed, she is sent to live with her grandmother on a wildlife reserve in Africa and discovers that the mysterious legends about a white giraffe are true.

🏆 **Stolz, Joelle.** *The Shadows of Ghadames.* Trans. Catherine Temerson. (Delacorte, 2004) 128p. **Libya.** 🔲 5–8 🔲 5.9. Batchelder Award

> Eleven-year-old Malika lives a quiet, secluded life with her strict Muslim family in nineteenth-century Ghadames, Libya. But her life changes when a stranger comes to stay with them.

Washington, Donna L. *A Pride of African Tales.* Illus. James Ransome (Amistad, 2003) 80p. **Ghana, Nigeria, Cameroon, Congo.** 🔲 1–5 🔲 3.9

> These six illustrated tales from different parts of Africa represent a range of cultures and genres.

Nonfiction

Brown, Don. *Uncommon Traveler: Mary Kingsley in Africa* (Houghton Mifflin, 2000) 32p. **Western Africa.** 🔲 K–4 🔲 3.3

> A picture book biography of the extraordinary English woman, Mary Kingsley, who traveled on her own through West Africa in 1893–1894.

Cowley, Joy. *Chameleon, Chameleon.* Photog. Nic Bishop (Scholastic, 2005) 32p. **Madagascar.** 🔲 K–4 🔲 1.7

> Follow the panther chameleon from Madagascar on a typical day, avoiding enemies, finding food, and flirting with a potential mate.

Croze, Harvey. *Africa for Kids: Exploring a Vibrant Continent, 19 Activities* (Chicago Review Press, 2006) 136p. **IL** 3–6 **RL** 4

The African continent is so big that three United States could fit on it. This book tells you all about the land, plants, animals, and people of Africa.

Deedy, Carmen Agra, and Wilson Kimeli Naiyomah. *14 Cows for America.* Illus. Thomas Gonzalez (Peachtree, 2009) 36p. **Kenya. IL** 2–5 **RL** 2.2

This true story describes a Kenyan Maasai tribe's generous response to the 2001 World Trade Center attack. Believing that "To heal a sorrowing heart, give something that is dear to your own," they joined together to give a special gift in the hopes that their compassion would take away some of the Americans' sadness.

Gibbons, Gail. *Elephants of Africa* (Holiday House, 2008) 32p. **IL** 1–4 **RL** 5.9

Everything you ever wanted to know about elephants is explained in this informative picture book.

Haas, Robert B. *African Critters* (National Geographic, 2002) 96p. **Southern Africa. IL** 3–6 **RL** 8.6

Follow a wildlife photographer in this virtual safari filled with true stories of African animals in the wild.

Joubert, Beverly, and Dereck Joubert. *Face to Face with Elephants* (National Geographic, 2008) 32p. **IL** 4–7 **RL** 5.7

Facts and true stories about elephants, as well as tips for protecting them. See also *Face to Face with Lions* (National Geographic, 2010).

Mandela, Nelson. Abridged by Chris Van Wyk. *Long Walk to Freedom.* Illus. Paddy Bouma (Roaring Brook, 2009) 57p. **South Africa. IL** 2–5 **RL** 4.5

This is the official abridged picture book version of Nelson Mandela's autobiography *Long Walk to Freedom*. It describes his childhood, education, and long struggle to create democracy in South Africa.

McDonough, Yona Zeldis. *Peaceful Protest: The Life of Nelson Mandela.* Illus. Malcah Zeldis (Walker, 2002) 32p. **South Africa. IL** 2–5 **RL** 4

This picture book biography tells the story of Nelson Mandela's early life, his twenty-seven years in jail and finally his election as president of the newly democratic South Africa in 1994.

Napoli, Donna Jo. *Mama Miti: Wengari Maathai and the Trees of Kenya.* Illus. Kadir Nelson (Simon & Schuster, 2010) 32p. **Kenya.** IL K–4 RL 3.4

This picture book biography of Wengari Muta Maathai highlights the various ways that planting trees in Kenya has improved the lives of the people there.

Sloan, Christopher. *SuperCroc and the Origin of Crocodiles* (National Geographic, 2002) 56p. **Niger.** IL 5–7 RL 6.5

In the Tenere Desert in Niger, scientists discovered the bones of a prehistoric crocodile that was almost as big as the *Tyrannosaurus rex.*

Thimmesh, Catherine. *Lucy Long Ago: Uncovering the Mystery of Where We Came From.* Illus. Oscar Sanisidro (Houghton Mifflin, 2009) 64p. **Ethiopia.** IL 5–9 RL 10.7

In 1974, scientists discovered the fossil bones of an undiscovered human species. This book describes how they put together the skeleton, determined where it belongs on the human family tree, and created a lifelike model of the hominid named "Lucy."

Turner, Pamela S. *Gorilla Doctors: Saving Endangered Great Apes* (Houghton Mifflin, 2005) 64p. **Rwanda, Uganda.** IL 4–8 RL 5.9

This book documents the work of the Mountain Gorilla Veterinary Project, a group of veterinarians who make "forest calls" to save the mountain gorilla population in Rwanda and Uganda.

Winter, Jeanette. *Wangari's Trees of Peace: A True Story from Africa* (Harcourt, 2008) 32p. **Kenya.** IL K–4 RL 4

A picture book biography of Wangari Maathai, environmentalist and winner of the Nobel Peace Prize, who started the Green Belt Movement in Kenya.

Grades 7 and Up—Fiction

🏆 **Coman, Carolyn.** *Many Stones* (Front Street, 2000) 158p. **South Africa.** IL YA RL 6.5. Printz Honor

Berry and her father travel together to South Africa for the memorial of Berry's sister Laura, who was murdered there.

Grades 7 and Up—Nonfiction

Lekuton, Joseph Lemasolai, with Herman Viola. *Facing the Lion: Growing Up Maasai on the African Savanna* (National Geographic, 2003) 127p. **Kenya.** ■ YA ■ 5.2

In nomadic Kenya, where the author grew up, Maasai children must choose between family duties or an education. This autobiography describes Joseph's childhood in Kenya until he leaves to go to college in America.

Chapter 2

Asia

China Booktalks

China's population is the largest in the world, despite its one-child policy established in 1979 to control the birth rate. Although the government still maintains strict political control over its citizens, reforms since the death of Chairman Mao have led to China's rising economic power and global prominence. Mao's devastating legacy—the Cultural Revolution in the 1960s that terrorized Chinese citizens and silenced a long heritage of art, education, and culture—is an important topic for young people to study, and the memoirs in this section make the topic immediate and engaging. The true stories of ancient Chinese emperors and their riches, the Great Wall, the Forbidden City, the mysterious terra cotta soldiers found in the emperor's tomb also make studying this country fun and exciting for kids. Although technically stories about the ancient Mongolian Empire do take place in what is now China, and Kublai Khan's famous palace was near the city of Beijing, those stories can be found in a separate section on Mongolia, Tibet, and Nepal.

Fiction

☗ Lin, Grace. *Where the Mountain Meets the Moon* (Little, Brown, 2009) 288p. **IL** 3–6 **RL** 5.4. Newbery Honor

This book can hook readers from the first sentence: "Far away from here, following the Jade River, there was once a black mountain that cut into the sky like a jagged piece of rough metal." Sounds like a pretty dismal place, and it turns out, it is. The villagers at the base of Fruitless Mountain were so poor, they could barely afford to eat. But one girl, Minli, is determined to help change her family's fortune. She meets a stranger selling goldfish, who promises that having a goldfish in her home will bring plenty of good fortune and gold. So Minli runs into her house and takes all the money they have to buy a goldfish. Of course, her mother is furious when she finds out, but Minli is about to discover that this is no ordinary fish. Minli is about to embark on an adventure involving dragons, emperors, gods and goddesses, and ancient stories that will change her life—and the lives of her family and village—and it will even change Fruitless Mountain itself.

McCaughrean, Geraldine. *The Kite Rider* (HarperCollins, 2001) 272p. **IL** 5–8 **RL** 6.2

When twelve-year-old Haoyou's father dies because of a dirty trick by a man named Di Chou, Haoyou wants to help support his mother. But they seem to be surrounded by evil people. Their uncle takes them in, but he is such a money-grubbing pig that when Di Chou asks to marry Haoyou's mother, Uncle agrees! Haoyou must find a way to get rid of Di Chou and support his mother on his own—but how? Finding the answer to that question takes him on an incredible adventure in which he goes blind in one eye, becomes friends with savage yurt-dwelling Mongols, and even meets the emperor Kublai Khan. If you like fast-paced historical adventure, you'll love this book.

Whelan, Gloria. *Chu Ju's House* (HarperCollins, 2004) 227p. **IL** 5–8 **RL** 5.2

Chu Ju is an only child living with her parents in China. Her mother is pregnant and they are all hoping the baby will be a boy. Girls are useless to their parents because when they grow up and get married, they go to live with the husband's parents and take care of his family. If Chu Ju's parents don't have a boy, then they will have no one to take care of them when they are old. The problem is, it's illegal to have more than two children in China, so if Chu Ju's mother has another girl, they have decided to send the baby away to an orphanage so they can still try again to have a son in the future.

When the baby is born and it's a girl, Chu Ju is so upset that she decides to run away so her baby sister won't have to grow up in a horrible orphanage. But that leaves Chu Ju out in the world all on her own. Where will she live? How will she get food? How will she survive? Read this book to find out.

🎬 Video Booktalk: http://www.bookwink.com/archive_2009_05_17.html

Nonfiction

Compestine, Ying Chang. *Revolution Is Not a Dinner Party* (Henry Holt, 2007) 256p. **IL** 5–9 **RL** 4

Imagine getting bullied in school because your father is a doctor and your clothes are nicer than everyone else's. Well, that's the least of Ling's problems when the Cultural Revolution sweeps China. Her father's best friend gets taken away by the police and is never heard from again. Her favorite aunt is taken out and humiliated in front of all her neighbors for being rich. Ling's father sticks up for her, saying that she never hurt anybody, but soon he is considered a class enemy, too. Their house gets ransacked; all their nice things are destroyed, and then, worst of all, Ling's father is arrested and taken away to prison. Based on true events from 1972 through 1976, this book shows readers what it was really like to live in Communist China during the Cultural Revolution.

Knox, Barbara. *Forbidden City: China's Imperial Palace* (Bearport, 2006) 32p. **IL** 4–7 **RL** 3.9

Emperors in ancient China were pretty cruel. They beat their servants and killed innocent messengers just for bringing them bad news. One of the cruelest and most hated emperors was Yung Lo, aka the Black Dragon. He didn't just want a royal palace; he wanted his own city, so he forced more than one million slaves and prisoners to build the Forbidden City in Beijing. It was called the Forbidden City because the only people allowed in were the emperor and his guests, plus the thousands of servants who catered to his every need. This book tells about the Forbidden City since it was built until today. Yes, it's still there today! Want to find out who lives there now? Read this book!

O'Connor, Jane. *The Emperor's Silent Army: Terracotta Warriors of Ancient China* (Viking, 2002) 48p. **IL** 4–6 **RL** 6.7

When you are an emperor, you don't have to play with tiny little army men. You can have artists create thousands of life-sized army men statues for you to position for battle. That's exactly what Qin Shihuang (pronounced chin shir-hwong) did in Ancient China. Only his statue army wasn't for play; it had a serious purpose. Qin Shihuang knew that when he died, his enemies would try to loot his tomb and steal all the valuable pearls, jade, and silk that would be buried with him, so to defend himself and his treasure in the afterlife, he had his statue army buried near his tomb and set up for battle. This book describes the armor, weapons, and positions of this amazing army created to defend the emperor's tomb.

Wenzel, Gregory. *Feathered Dinosaurs of China* (Charlesbridge, 2004) 32p. **IL** 4–6 **RL** 6.4

Imagine a typical day in the Liaoning Province of northeastern China—124 million years ago. Scientists have recently made discoveries there of layers upon layers of perfectly preserved fossils that give us incredibly detailed clues about what life was like during the Early Cretaceous Period. This book recreates the prehistoric ecosystem and makes you feel like you're there for a typical day with the dinosaurs and other life you would see on a hike near the lakes. Some animals you will recognize—frogs, dragonflies, fish, and turtles. And some you can only imagine, like the Jinzhousaurus, a giant twenty-foot long herbivore, the Sinorithosaurus, an eagle-like feathered hunter, and flying reptiles called pterosaurs. This book takes you on a fascinating journey through the forest and under water to the bottom of the lake to see what life was like for these prehistoric creatures.

China Book List

Ancient Chinese legends continue to inspire fantasy stories such as Grace Lin's Newbery Honor–winning *Where the Mountain Meets the Moon*. But the nonfiction represented in this list are also fun topics for kids: Chinese New Year, Confucius, and pandas!

Fiction

Grindley, Sally. *Spilled Water* (Bloomsbury, 2004) 224p. **IL** 4–7 **RL** 5

On the day that her uncle takes her to be sold to the highest bidder, eleven-year-old Lu Si-Yan learns what it means to be born a girl in her culture. She is taken to the big city where she will become a servant to a wealthy family, but Lu Si-Yan is determined to escape and find her way home.

Mowll, Joshua. *Operation Red Jericho.* Illus. Joshua Mowll, Julek Heller, and Niroot Puttapipat (Candlewick, 2005) 288p. **IL** 6–9 **RL** 6.8

While trying to find their missing parents, Doug and Becca encounter an ancient order of Chinese mercenaries, a brutal pirate warlord, a feisty Texan heiress, and a stolen cache of a volatile explosive called zoridium. By their saga's end, the duo has exposed a murderous plot involving their parents and uncovered a secret society hidden from the world for hundreds of years. See also the other books in the Guild of Specialists trilogy.

Noyes, Deborah. *Red Butterfly: How a Princess Smuggled the Secret of Silk Out of China.* Illus. Sophie Blackall (Candlewick, 2007) 32p. **IL** K–4 **RL** 5.6

In this picture book, a young Chinese princess is sent from her father's kingdom to marry the king of a far-off land. She begs her father to let her stay, but he insists that she go and fulfill her destiny as the queen of Khotan.

Pennypacker, Sara. *Sparrow Girl.* Illus. Yoko Tanaka (Hyperion, 2009) 40p. **IL** K–4 **RL** 2.3

This picture book dramatizes true events of 1958 when Chairman Mao ordered people to kill the entire sparrow population in China.

Russell, Ching Yeung. *Tofu Quilt* (Lee & Low, 2009) 136p. **IL** 4–6 **RL** 4

This novel in verse is based on the author's childhood in 1960s Hong Kong and her dreams of becoming a writer, despite the conventions of society.

Stone, Jeff. *The Five Ancestors: Tiger* (Random House, 2005) 208p. **IL** 6–9 **RL** 5.2

Twelve-year-old Fu doesn't know who his parents were. Raised by his grandmaster, he thinks of the temple as his home and his fellow warrior monks as his family of temple brothers. Then one terrible night, the temple is destroyed. Charged by their grandmaster to uncover the secrets of their past, the five temple brothers flee into the countryside. See also the other books in The Five Ancestors series.

Wilkinson, Carole. *Dragon Keeper* (Hyperion, 2005) 339p. **IL** 5–9 **RL** 5.3

An orphan slave girl named Ping and an endangered dragon race to escape an evil dragon hunter. See also the sequels *Garden of the Purple Dragon* (Hyperion, 2007) and *Dragon Moon* (Hyperion, 2008).

Nonfiction

Demi. *Su Dongpo: Chinese Genius* (Lee & Low, 2006) 32p. **IL** 4–7 **RL** 7.5

This is a picture book biography of Su Dongpo, eleventh-century Chinese poet, civil engineer, and statesman.

Dowson, Nick. *Tracks of a Panda.* Illus. Yu Rong (Candlewick, 2007) 32p. **IL** K–4 **RL** 6

In this picture book, a mother panda teaches her cub how to survive in their mountain habitat.

Freedman, Russell. *Confucius: The Golden Rule.* Illus. Frederic Clement (Arthur A. Levine, 2002) 48p. **IL** 4–8 **RL** 5.9

This picture book biography depicts the life of Confucius, the great Chinese teacher and philosopher who lived five centuries before Jesus and is famous for professing the Golden Rule: "Do not impose on others what you do not wish for yourself."

Gibbons, Gail. *Giant Pandas* (Holiday House, 2002) 32p. **IL** 1–4 **RL** 3.9

Learn all about the life and behavior of panda bears in China with this picture book.

Jango-Cohen, Judith. *Chinese New Year.* Illus. Jason Chin (Carolrhoda, 2005) 48p. **IL** 1–4 **RL** 2.3

This picture book describes the celebration of the Chinese New Year, including the Chinese zodiac, traditional symbols of the New Year, family feasts and traditions, and parades.

Platt, Richard. *Through Time: Beijing.* Illus. Capon Manuela (Kingfisher, 2008) 48p. **IL** 3–7 **RL** 5.3

Follow the rise and fall of great dynasties and the everyday lives of the citizens who prospered or suffered under their rule. Beginning in prehistoric times, this book tells the story of Beijing—its triumphs, conflicts, and people—right up to the present day.

Rumford, James. *Chee-Lin: A Giraffe's Journey* (Houghton Mifflin, 2008) 40p. **IL** 1–4 **RL** 3

Beautifully illustrated and based on the life of a real giraffe in the 1400s, this picture book tells the story of the first giraffe ever to visit China.

Yu, Chun. *Little Green: Growing Up in the Cultural Revolution* (Simon & Schuster, 2005) 128p. **IL** 5–9 **RL** 5.5

    In this autobiography told in free verse, the author describes her childhood during the Chinese Cultural Revolution.

Grades 7 and Up—Fiction

Namioka, Lensey. *Ties That Bind, Ties That Break* (Delacorte, 1999) 154p. **IL** YA **RL** 6.3

    Ailin's life takes a different turn when she defies the traditions of upper-class Chinese society by refusing to have her feet bound.

Grades 7 and Up—Nonfiction

Jiang, Ji-li. *Red Scarf Girl: A Memoir of the Cultural Revolution* (HarperCollins, 1997) 285p. **IL** YA **RL** 6.1

    In 1966, the year that China's leader launches the Cultural Revolution, twelve-year-old Ji-li's world begins to fall apart. This is the true story of one girl's determination to hold her family together during this terrifying era of the twentieth century.

Li, Moying. *Snow Falling in Spring: Coming of Age in China During the Cultural Revolution* (FSG, 2008) 176p. **IL** YA **RL** 8.6

    Moying describes her true story of the chaos and brutality that came with the Cultural Revolution in the late 1960s.

Ma, Adeline Yen. *Chinese Cinderella: The True Story of an Unwanted Daughter* (Delacorte, 1999) 205p. **IL** YA **RL** 6.8

    In this memoir of her childhood, Adeline's affluent, powerful family considers her bad luck after her mother dies giving birth to her, and her life does not get any easier when her father remarries.

India, Pakistan, and Bangladesh Booktalks

    India is one of the fastest growing economies in the world, yet it still suffers from extreme wealth inequality, poverty, disease, and malnutrition. India, Pakistan, and Bangladesh offer a tremendous range of teachable topics, from the extreme poverty of the slums and the injustice of forced child labor to the extravagant opulence of royalty and the Taj Mahal. These books also show the strict gender expectations the society put on girls in the past, highlighting the difference in personal freedom, education, and economic independence between boys and girls.

Fiction

Doder, Joshua. *Grk Smells a Rat* (Random House, 2008) 202p. **India.** **IL** 4–7 **RL** 3.5

If you're familiar with the other books in the <u>Grk</u> series, then you know that Tim lives with his dog Grk and their two friends, Max and Natascha Raffifi. How they all came to live together is a long story, and you'll have to read *A Dog Called Grk* if you really want to know. But you don't have to read it to understand this book, in which Tim and his family are visiting India for a tennis tournament that Max is playing in. While they are there, Tim uncovers a dangerous gang of criminals who kidnap children to put into slavery. He meets a boy named Krishnan, who begs Tim to help rescue his sister from a life of forced labor with the Blue Rat Gang, but Tim is just a tourist. What can he do? Well, he and Natascha decide to try to help, but they have no idea who they are dealing with and get in way over their heads. Luckily, their dog Grk is very intelligent and brave and manages to save them all. If you like fast-paced books with danger and adventure, plus a brave and intelligent dog, then you will love this and the other books in the <u>Grk</u> series.

♈Perkins, Mitali. *Rickshaw Girl.* Illus. Jamie Hogan (Charlesbridge, 2007) 91p. **Bangladesh.** **IL** 2–5 **RL** 4. Jane Addams Honor

Naima's father is a rickshaw driver. A rickshaw is like a bicycle taxi, and people pay him to take them places so they don't have to walk. It is very tiring work, but their family really needs the money. Naima wishes she could drive the rickshaw so her father could take a break, but girls are not allowed to work outside of the home. They are supposed to stay home and help their mothers. So driving a rickshaw is not in Naima's future, but she is a really good artist. With her artistic ability, maybe there is some way she can help her family to earn money.

Qamar, Amjed. *Beneath My Mother's Feet* (Atheneum, 2008) 198p. **Pakistan.** **IL** 6–9 **RL** 4.3

Nazia lives in Pakistan with her family, and she has always been a good, obedient daughter. She does well in school, and soon she will marry the person her parents chose for her—whether she likes him or not. But when her father breaks his leg and can't work, Nazia's sheltered life gradually falls apart. First her mother takes her out of school to work all day as a housecleaner so they can make enough money to pay the rent. Nazia hates it, but at least she's going to get married soon and leave. Then her brother steals her dowry and runs away, meaning Nazia will have to work even longer to save money before she can get married. Then their rent money is stolen and the landlord kicks them out. Now Nazia has no school, no dowry, and no place to live. Worse, when her future in-laws find out that she is a now a servant, they cancel the wedding. What will she do now? She has always done what her parents wanted. Aren't they supposed to be taking care of her? Nazia realizes that she will have to take care of herself and decide how to live her own life, even if it means disobeying her parents.

Sheth, Kashmira. *Keeping Corner* (Hyperion, 2007) 281p. **India.** ⒣ 6–9 ⒭ 4.3

Throughout history in India, girls have relied on tradition to tell them what to do. Their parents choose their husbands for them and decide when the girl is old enough to get married. If a husband dies before his wife, then tradition tells the woman what she can and can't do. She can't wear any jewelry or any colors, only white clothes. She has to shave her head, and she has to stay inside the house for a whole year to "keep corner." So imagine being twelve years old and being engaged to a boy you barely know—then he dies. Your life is pretty much over, too. That's what happens to Leela in this story. She has to give up her beautiful clothes, jewelry, and hair (!) and she can't go out for an entire year! How does she survive without going crazy? Read this book to find out.

Venkarraman, Padma. *Climbing the Stairs* (Putnam, 2008) 247p. **India.** ⒣ 6–9 ⒭ 4.3

Vidya is a fifteen-year-old girl who dreams of going to college—not a typical option for a girl in 1940s India. She adores her father, but when he gets beat up by police in a riot against the British rule, he is never the same again. Vidya and her family have to go live with her grandparents in a much more strict and traditional household. While there, she spends as much time as possible reading in her grandfather's library, and she also becomes friends with a boy named Rattan, who wants more than friendship from her. Will Vidya give up her dream of college and take the safe traditional path of marriage?

Whelan, Gloria. *Homeless Bird* (HarperCollins, 2000) 192p. **India.** ⒣ 4–8 ⒭ 6.1

In India, girls weren't allowed to earn money for themselves. The strict tradition said they had to marry the boy their parents chose, then go to live with his family and basically be a servant for the mother-in-law for the rest of their lives. When thirteen-year-old Koly gets married, that's all she expects out of her life. But her husband has tuberculosis and dies shortly after their wedding, and Koly is a widow, completely dependent on her in-laws to support her. On a trip to Delhi, the mother-in-law abandons Koly, and she is alone out on the streets with no one to help her. But what at first seems like a tragedy turns out to be the best thing that could ever happen because Koly learns how to survive on her own and have a better life than she ever would have before.

Nonfiction

Ali, Rubina. *Slumgirl Dreaming: Rubina's Journey to the Stars* (Delacorte, 2009) 188p. **India.** **IL** 4–7 **RL** 4.7

This is the true story of a nine-year-old girl who lives in a slum in India. There are millions of kids like her who live in rat-infested shacks with no electricity and no running water, surrounded by stinking piles of garbage and poo. But Rubina Ali is different because she was lucky enough to be cast in a movie called *Slumdog Millionaire.* This book is her autobiography, and she describes her life in the slum, her family, and what it was like to audition and be chosen for the movie. She describes what it was like to film her scenes, go to America for the Academy Awards (the movie won the Oscar for Best Picture in 2008), and then have to return home to her slum. It's an amazing story. If you have ever dreamed of being in a movie, then you will love this book.

Arnold, Caroline, and Madeleine Comora. *Taj Mahal.* Illus. Rahul Bhushan (Carolrhoda, 2007) 32p. **India.** **IL** 4–7 **RL** 6

The Taj Mahal in Agra, India, is one of the seven man-made wonders of the world. It is a symbol of Indian architecture, like the Pyramids are to ancient Egypt and the Eiffel Tower is to Paris. But how was it created, and why? According to legend, it was built as a tomb for the emperor's wife to be a monument to universal love. Can you imagine loving someone enough to build a huge palace like that? Well, actually, the emperor didn't build it himself. He had the best workers and materials brought in from all over Asia, and it took them eleven years to complete it. Read about the legendary love story, and about the construction of the spectacular palace.

Montgomery, Sy. *The Man-Eating Tigers of Sundarbans.* Photog. Eleanor Briggs (Houghton Mifflin, 2001) 57p. **India, Bangladesh.** **IL** 4–9 **RL** 6.4

In Africa, lions are king of the jungle, but in India, no animal is more feared than the tiger. No other predator kills more humans per year than the Royal Bengal tiger, not even sharks. This book takes you into the heart of man-eating tiger country, the Sundarbans (pronounced SHUN-dar-buns). It's a flooded forest on the coast of the Bay of Bengal. Here the tigers are so stealthy, you won't hear them or see them before they grab you by the back of the neck and carry you off for dinner. This book tells you all about the Royal Bengal tigers—how they hunt, why they attack humans, and what to do if you come across one. (Hint: don't run!)

India, Pakistan, and Bangladesh Book List

The overarching theme of all these books for me is extreme sensory overload. The books in this list feel positively frenetic with colors and sounds, smells and tastes of spicy food, heavy rain, and soggy, sticky heat. Perfect for making kids feel like they are right there in this fascinating part of the world!

Fiction

D'Amamo, Francesco. *Iqbal* (Atheneum, 2003) 120p. **Pakistan.** **IL** 4–7 **RL** 4

This book is based on the real life of Iqbal Masih, a child activist in Pakistan who ran away from the carpet factory where he was forced to work to pay off his parents' debts.

Divakaruni, Chitra Banerjee. *The Conch Bearer* (Roaring Brook, 2003) 265p. **India.** **IL** 4–7 **RL** 6.5

In India, twelve-year-old Anand discovers his destiny as the bearer of a magical and powerful conch shell, but must make sure it doesn't fall into enemy hands. See also the sequels *The Mirror of Fire and Dreaming* (Roaring Brook, 2005) and *Shadowland* (Roaring Brook, 2009).

Shea, Pegi Deitz. *The Carpet Boy's Gift.* Illus. Leane Morin (Tilbury House, 2003) 40p. **Pakistan.** **IL** 2–5 **RL** 4

This picture book illustrates the practice of child labor in carpet factories and provides a list of extra resources for more information about protecting children's rights.

Sheth, Kashmira. *Boys without Names* (Baltzer + Bray, 2010) 320p. **India.** **IL** 4–7 **RL** 4.2

This harrowing story highlights the plight of poverty and child slave labor. Eleven-year-old Gopal tries to help his family but ends up trapped working in a sweatshop under horrible conditions.

Singh, Vandana. *Younguncle Comes to Town.* Illus. B. M. Kamath (Viking, 2004) 153p. **India.** **IL** 3–5 **RL** 5.7

In a small town in modern India, a family has some funny new adventures when their eccentric uncle comes to live with them.

Staples, Suzanne Fisher. *The House of Djinn* (FSG, 2008) 207p. **Pakistan.** **IL** 6–9 **RL** 6

Shabanu's daughter, Mumtaz, and nephew, Jameel, both aged fifteen, are caught between ancient Pakistani traditions and modern Western ideas. See also *Shabanu: Daughter of the Wind* (Knopf, 1989) and *Haveli* (Knopf, 1993).

Staples, Suzanne Fisher. *Under the Persimmon Tree* (FSG, 2005) 275p. **Pakistan.** **IL** 6–9 **RL** 7.1

Najmal, a young refugee from the war in Afghanistan, meets a Muslim American teacher at a school in Peshawar, Pakistan.

Nonfiction

Demi. *Gandhi* (Simon & Schuster, 2001) 36p. **India.** **IL** 4–7 **RL** 5.9

A picture book biography of the amazing leader who brought about change in India through nonviolent protest.

Hatkoff, Craig, Isabella Hatkoff, and Juliana Hatkoff, *Leo the Snow Leopard: The True Story of an Amazing Rescue* (Scholastic, 2010) 40p. **Pakistan.** **IL** K–5 **RL** 5.9

This picture book depicts the true story of an orphaned snow leopard who was rescued in Himalayan Pakistan and sent to the Bronx Zoo.

Heiligman, Deborah. *Celebrate Diwali: With Sweets, Lights, and Fireworks* (National Geographic, 2006) 32p. **India.** **IL** 1–4 **RL** 2.9

This picture book describes the food and festivities of the Indian Festival of Lights—Diwali.

Heydlauff, Lisa. *Going to School in India.* Photog. Nitin Upadyhe (Charlesbridge, 2005) 98p. **India.** **IL** 3–5 **RL** 4

Inspiring stories of children all across India who go to school—sometimes against great odds—to pursue their dreams.

Mortenson, Greg, and David Oliver Relin. *Three Cups of Tea: One Man's Journey to Change the World . . . One Child at a Time* (Dial, 2009) 205p. **Pakistan.** **IL** 6–8 **RL** 5.9

This edition has been specially adapted for younger readers to tell the remarkable true story of an American man who pledged to build a school for children in Pakistan. See also the picture book version of the same story, *Listen to the Wind: The Story of Dr. Greg and Three Cups of Tea* (Dial, 2009).

Grades 7 and Up—Fiction

Y Michaelis, Antonia. *Tiger Moon* (Amulet, 2008) 448p. **India.** **IL** YA **RL** 5.4. Batchelder Honor

The Hindu god Krishna chooses an unlikely hero to journey through India on an enchanted tiger to rescue a kidnapped princess from becoming the bride of a demon king.

Perkins, Mitali. *Monsoon Summer* (Delacorte, 2004) 257p. **India.** **IL** YA **RL** 4.3

A California teenager spends the summer in India and learns about love, friendship, and herself.

Perkins, Mitali. *Secret Keeper* (Delacorte, 2009) 225p. **India.** **IL** YA **RL** 4.8

Osh and her sister Reet go with their mother to live with their father's brother and his family when their own father leaves for America to find a job, promising to send for them as soon as he can.

Sheth, Kashmira. *Koyal Dark, Mango Sweet* (Hyperion, 2006) 224p. **India.** **IL** YA **RL** 4.5

In modern-day Mumbai, India, sixteen-year-old Jeeta disagrees with much of her mother's traditional advice about how to live her life.

Tomlinson, Heather. *Toads and Diamonds* (Henry Holt, 2010) 288p. India **IL** YA **RL** 5.4

A retelling of a classical fairy tale set in a magical Indian world.

Southeast Asia Booktalks

This section paints a broad picture of Southeastern Asia, with books representing life in several countries including Burma (Myanmar), Cambodia, Thailand, Vietnam, Malaysia, and Indonesia. The climate is hot and wet with seasonal monsoons, perfect for rice paddy agriculture and for water-loving elephants. Kids will be fascinated to learn from these books what an important role elephants play in people's everyday lives in these countries.

Fiction

Fleischman, Sid. *The White Elephant.* Illus. Robert McGuire (Greenwillow, 2006) 95p. **Thailand.** ▦ 3–5 ▧ 4.3

A white elephant sale is another word for a flea market, where people try to get rid of their unwanted stuff. This book tells the Thai legend of how that expression came about. The main character, Run-Run, is an elephant driver, and he loves his elephant Walking Mountain, but one day Walking Mountain gets him into big trouble with the prince. He is having fun and spraying water with his trunk on the kids in the street, when the prince rides by and gets a whole trunk full of water poured on him. The prince is so angry that he decides to send Run-Run a gift that will curse him until the end of his days. He sends Run-Run a white elephant named Sahib. Why is that such a curse? Well, this elephant is sacred; he can never work. He needs special expensive food. He must be treated like an honored guest or the prince will be furious. But Sahib has his own ideas about how he wants to live, and Run-Run has his hands full trying to control him. If you like funny books about animals, you'll love *The White Elephant.*

Ho, Minfong. *The Stone Goddess* (Orchard, 2003) 201p. **Cambodia.** ▦ 6–9 ▧ 5.9

Nakri is twelve years old during the Vietnam War when the Communist Khmer Rouge party takes over Cambodia. Nakri and her family, afraid of being bombed by the Americans, leave their home in Phnom Penh to go live in the country. But when they get there, they realize that life with the Communists is not any safer. Adults like Nakri's father, who have an education and good jobs, are suspected of being traitors, and many are taken away and never seen again. Nakri and her brother and sister are sent to live in a labor camp where they are forced to work in the rice fields and are given hardly any food to eat. This book is fiction but is based on the true stories of survivors of the "killing fields" of Cambodia, and it makes you feel what life must have been like during that horrible time.

Lewis, Richard. *The Killing Sea* (Simon & Schuster, 2006) 183p. **Indonesia.** **IL** 6–9 **RL** 4.3

On December 26, 2004, an earthquake in the Indian Ocean caused a tsunami that hit Indonesia and several other countries with coastlines on the Indian Ocean. The ground on the ocean floor shifted, and all that water went rushing away toward the coast in a wave train over 100 feet high. This book is a fictional account of that day in a town in Banda Aceh, Indonesia. It tells the story of three kids, Ruslan, a local Indonesian boy, and Sarah and Peter, American tourists who get separated from their parents when the wave hits. It describes the death, destruction, and fear the people experienced, and the fight for survival afterward with disease, hunger, terrorism and crime rampant during the chaos. For Sarah and Peter, it is especially scary because they are on their own in a foreign country where they don't speak the language. When Peter gets sick, they know he won't survive without help, but with nothing but destruction all around, who can help them?

Marsden, Carolyn. *When Heaven Fell* (Candlewick, 2007) 183p. **Vietnam.** **IL** 3–5 **RL** 3.9

Binh is a nine-year-old girl living with her family in Vietnam. It is thirty years after the war, and life is peaceful, but they are still very poor—so poor that the kids in Binh's family can't go to school. Even though it only costs about forty dollars a year, the family just can't afford the extra expense, and the children are needed at home to work. You might not think school is great, but it's better than having to work all day. So Binh is really excited when she finds out that her grandmother had another baby during the war but had to give her up for adoption to a family in the United States. In the movies, everyone in America is rich! Maybe her American aunt will take her back to live with her, and then Binh can be rich, too. But when they meet the American lady, she is not at all what they had expected or hoped.

Smith, Roland. *Elephant Run* (Hyperion, 2007) 318p. **Burma.** **IL** 5–8 **RL** 4.3

Nick Freestone lives with his divorced mother in London in 1941, but when the Germans start bombing heavily, she decides that Nick would be safer if he lived with his father in the British colony of Burma. So Nick travels to his father's teak plantation in the Asian tropics. The plantation has been in Nick's family for generations, and one day Nick will inherit it and be the boss of all the Burmese mahouts, the elephant riders, who work on the plantation. Or so he thinks. But if Nick's mother thought he would be safe from the war there, she could not have been more wrong. On Nick's second day in Burma, the Japanese attack. They take over the plantation, making it their headquarters, and they separate the prisoners. Nick's father and the Burmese who are loyal to him are forced to march to a work camp thousands of miles away. The Japanese colonel takes pity on Nick and allows him to stay at the plantation as a servant. Nick's father promises to somehow escape and come rescue him, but he knows that the Japanese soldiers are so brutal, many prisoners don't even survive, much less escape. Nick's only hope is to escape on his own, but that is a very slim hope. Will he be able to do it? Read this book to find out.

Nonfiction

Buchmann, Stephen, and Diana Cohn. *The Bee Tree.* Illus. Paul Mirocha (Cinco Puntos, 2007) 40p. **Malaysia. IL** 3–6 **RL** 8.3

In Malaysia there are giant trees in the rainforest, some as tall as a thirty-story skyscraper. Migrating honeybees build their nests in these trees every year, and amazingly brave Malaysians called honey hunters climb the trees to steal the honey. Imagine climbing up a tree 250 feet in the air to stick your hands into a bees' nest filled with tens of thousands of angry bees! How do you think they do it without getting stung a million times and falling to their deaths? Read this true picture book story to find out.

Goldenberg, Linda. *Little People and a Lost World: An Anthropological Mystery* (Twenty-First Century, 2007) 112p. **Indonesia. IL** 4–8 **RL** 8.6

In a remote cave on a small island in Indonesia, archaeologists made an extraordinary discovery: the skeleton of a three-foot-tall adult that was eighteen thousand years old, older than Neanderthal humans! This book describes all the questions that scientists are trying to answer about this discovery. Were all the adults tiny back then, or did this one have some kind of disease? How did these little people hunt and kill the giant Komodo dragons and stegodons, whose bones were also found in the cave? How did people even get to this island in the first place? There was no land bridge connecting the islands in the past. Did they build rafts to float across the ocean from the mainland? Then there is the question of how long they lived there, and this is where the story gets strange. On this island in Indonesia, there are legends about a civilization of little people living there as late as the nineteenth century! Is it possible that this three-foot tall prehistoric species was living at the same time as modern humans? That would be like seeing a dinosaur walking down the street. Scientists don't have the answers to these questions, but this book is a fascinating look at some of their theories so far about this exciting new discovery.

Montgomery, Sy. *Search for the Golden Moon Bear: Science and Adventure in the Asian Tropics* (Houghton Mifflin, 2004) 80p. **Cambodia.** **IL** 5–9 **RL** 6

For almost twenty years, Cambodia was so dangerous with wars, terrorists, and land mines that no foreigners dared to go there. This was terrible for the people of Cambodia, who starved, were murdered, or were maimed by exploding land mines, but it was a good thing for the plants and animals of Cambodia, which were basically left alone while the people dealt with their own problems. But in the late 1990s, when it was safer for outsiders to visit Cambodia, scientists from other parts of the world started discovering brand-new species that had never been seen before. This book is about one possible new species called the Golden Moon Bear. An American scientist had seen a strange golden orange bear in a cage and wanted to know if it was a whole new species or just a freak. This book describes how they traveled to Cambodia and Thailand to find the answer, and how the answer might help protect all Asian bears. If you're interested in science, DNA, and wildlife conservation, you'll be fascinated by this book.

Southeast Asia Book List

Kids studying twentieth-century history will find books about the Vietnam War here and also books about the Cambodian holocaust in which 2 million people died under the brutal Khmer Rouge government.

Fiction

Kadohata, Cynthia. *Cracker!: The Best Dog in Vietnam* (Atheneum, 2007) 320p. **Vietnam.** **IL** 5–8 **RL** 4

A German shepherd named Cracker trains to become an army dog for the Vietnam War.

Kadohata, Cynthia. *A Million Shades of Gray* (Atheneum, 2010) 224p. **Vietnam.** IL 6–9 RL 4.3

    In 1975, a thirteen-year-old boy and his beloved elephant escape into the jungle when the Viet Cong attack his Vietnamese village.

Lipp, Frederick. *Running Shoes.* Illus. Jason Gallard (Charlesbridge, 2007) 32p. **Cambodia.** IL K–4 RL 3

    In this picture book, a girl living in a remote village in Cambodia has a secret wish to go to school, but she can't walk the eight kilometers to the nearest school in bare feet. She needs running shoes to make her dream come true.

Marsden, Carolyn, and Thay Phap Niem. *The Buddha's Diamonds* (Candlewick, 2008) 106p. **Vietnam.** IL 4–7 RL 3.9

    When a storm comes and damages the family's fishing boat on the coast of Vietnam, Tinh has to grow up and learn more responsibility.

Myers, Walter Dean. *Patrol: An American Soldier in Vietnam.* Illus. Ann Grifalconi (HarperCollins, 2002) 40p. **Vietnam.** IL 3–7 RL 3.1

    This picture book explores the fear and other emotions of an American soldier in Vietnam.

Vander Zee, Ruth. *Always with You.* Illus. Ronald Himler (Eerdmans, 2008) 32p. **Vietnam.** IL 3–4 RL 2.9

    In this picture book, Kim is four years old when her village in Vietnam is bombed and she is sent to live in an orphanage.

Nonfiction

Lord, Michelle. *A Song for Cambodia.* Illus. Shino Arihara (Lee & Low, 2008) 32p. **Cambodia.** IL 3–5 RL 5

    In this picture book retelling of a true story, a young boy who was separated from his parents during the reign of the Khmer Rouge in Cambodia barely survives the work camps until he escapes as a refugee to Thailand.

Morris, Ann, and Heidi Larson. *Tsunami: Helping Each Other* (Millbrook, 2005) 32p. **Thailand.** ⬛ 3–6 ⬛ 8.3

This book includes photographs and text to show how people in a coastal area of Thailand coped with the devastating effects of the 2004 tsunami.

Reynolds, Jan. *Cycle of Rice, Cycle of Life: A Story of Sustainable Farming* (Lee & Low, 2009) 48p. **Indonesia.** ⬛ 5–9 ⬛ 10

This photo essay explores the cultural and environmental aspects of traditional Balinese rice farming, a model of sustainable food production.

Sobol, Richard. *An Elephant in the Backyard* (Dutton, 2004) 32p. **Thailand.** ⬛ K–4 ⬛ 4.5

This photo-essay describes what life is like for elephants in the village of Tha Kleng in Thailand and the children who grow up alongside them.

Japan and Korea Booktalks

Both Japan and Korea were in complete isolation from the rest of the world until the nineteenth century. They preferred to have no contact with other countries. But the late nineteenth century brought changes to both countries, and Japan forcibly occupied Korea during the early twentieth century until World War II. Now, of course, they are both modern economic powers. Japan is the world's third largest economy, and Korea hosted the World Cup in 2002. But they remain proud of their traditions and culture that they worked so hard to protect from being contaminated by the outside world. The books in this section should give young readers a taste of the rich heritage of these two countries.

Fiction

Holman, Sheri. *Sondok, Princess of the Moon and Stars: Korea, A.D. 595* (Scholastic, 2002) 187p. **Korea.** ⬛ 3–6 ⬛ 5.9

Lady Sondok is heir to the throne of Silla, now called Korea. She is fascinated with astronomy and loves nothing better than to be outside at night studying the moon and stars. So she is really excited when she finds out that an educated ambassador from China is coming to visit. She really wants to talk to him about astronomy and find out what they know in China. But when Lord Lin Fang comes and presents his astronomical calendar to her father, the ruler, there is a mistake in the Chinese calculations. It predicts a solar eclipse on the wrong day. Eclipses were a big deal back then, and getting it wrong would make the ruler look very dumb in front of his people. Sondok does the calculations over and over again. She knows the Chinese calendar is wrong, but Lord Lin Fang refuses to speak to her because she is a girl. He finds it appalling that a girl should study serious subjects like mathematics and astronomy, much less rule a country! Slowly Lin Fang starts to influence her father and convince him that Sondok should act more like a proper lady. One by one all the things she loves are taken away from her, first her astronomy, and then her best friend, and finally even her mother is replaced because she was never able to have a son. This story is based on the real-life queen Sondok who did eventually rule in what is now the southeast part of Korea (and build her own observatory for studying the stars).

Lasky, Kathryn. *Kazunomiya: Prisoner of Heaven, Japan 1858* (Scholastic, 2004) 156p. Japan. IL 4–8 RL 5.6

Princess Kazunomiya is twelve years old, and because she is the emperor's half-sister, she lives in the Imperial Palace with the rest of the courtiers. All descendents of the emperor are considered gods, and their palace is called the Heavenly Palace, but Kazunomiya thinks it is more like a prison because she can never leave or even have any say over what happens in her life. Since she was four years old, she has been engaged to marry Prince Arisugawa, and as she gets older, she is starting to fall in love with him and look forward to their marriage. But the political situation in Japan is changing, and the emperor needs to make an alliance with the powerful shogun warriors, so he arranges for Kazunomiya to marry Yoshitomi, the future shogun of Japan. Not only that, but they want to change her birthday to make it more lucky for this new marriage. Nothing in her life is hers anymore! Her Auntie feels sorry for her and arranges secret meetings between Kazunomiya and her love Arisugawa. But how will it end? Will Kazunomiya be a puppet all her life, or will she be able to marry the man the she loves? Read this book to find out.

Meehan, Kieran. *Hannah's Winter* (Kane Miller, 2009) 212p. Japan. IL 5–8 RL 4

Hannah's mother brings her from their home in Australia to stay with her friends in Osaka, Japan, for the "cultural experience." Hannah is not sure she wants a new cultural experience, but when she gets there, she becomes friends with the daughter her age, Miki, and they end up having a really great time. Strange things start happening as soon as Hannah shows up, however, and the girls find a mysterious message in the stationery shop. The first strange thing that happens is when Hannah looks in the mirror one day and doesn't see her own face; instead, she sees a ship sailing in the distance. Freaky! They realize that there is a ghost in the house, and he is trying to tell Hannah something with that mysterious message. Honestly, the ghost part was not scary. It all got wrapped up pretty easily and predictably. The details about Japan, the food, the landscape, and the culture are so exciting to read about. It really makes you want to go there!

O'Brien, Anne Sibley. *The Legend of Hong Kil Dong: The Robin Hood of Korea* (Charlesbridge, 2006) 48p. **Korea.** ▮ 3–7 ▮ 3.7

If you know the Robin Hood story about the men who secretly steal from the rich to give to the poor, then the story in this graphic novel will be familiar to you. Hong Kil Dong is the son of a powerful government official in Korea, but because his mother is a commoner, Kil Dong's father can't pass on his position to him. Only the child of two noble parents can inherit the status of the parents and serve in the government. So even though Kil Dong is smart, strong, and good, he will have to make his own way in the world without any help from his powerful father. He goes to a monastery in the mountains to study with the monks and hopefully figure out his destiny. While there, he meets a mysterious old sage who trains him in martial arts and ancient magic until his skill and strength are greater than anyone's in the land. Still not sure of his destiny, Kil Dong is challenged by a group of bandits in the forest. Kil Dong beats them easily, and they kowtow to him as their leader. He trains them into a fighting force, and they start helping the poor people, who are overtaxed by the greedy nobles. But of course, the nobles all across the land want to catch Kil Dong. How long can he keep doing his good work when there is a huge reward for his capture?

☗ Uehashi, Nahoko. *Moribito: Guardian of the Spirit.* Trans. Cathy Hirano. Illus. Yuko Shimizu (Arthur A. Levine, 2008) 248p. **Japan.** ▮ 5–9 ▮ 5. Batchelder Award

Every one hundred years, the Water Spirit lays an egg inside a human. If this egg does not hatch, then there will be a terrible drought in the Nayoro Peninsula—the rice won't grow, and the people will starve. So the human carrying this egg has a very important job. That human is called the Moribito, the guardian of the spirit. But the Water Spirit doesn't come out and tell you about the egg; you have to rely on people who remember the stories of what happened from a hundred years ago to recognize the signs. That's the problem in this book. Chagum is the second prince of New Yogo, but he is acting strange, as if he were possessed. His father, the Mikado, can't risk the welfare of the country by having a prince who's possessed, so he arranges to have Chagum assassinated, making it look like an accident. But Chagum survives, and his mother realizes that he is in danger. She secretly hires the bodyguard, Balsa, to take away her son and hide him. They are tracked by the Mikado's men, and along the way, they realize that Chagum is the Moribito. It's more important than ever to protect him so that the egg he carries can hatch safely. Try this book if you like stories with magic, adventure, and lots of martial art fights (and it's not just boys either—the girls in this book kick butt, too!). See also the Batchelder Honor–winning sequel *Moribito II: Guardian of the Darkness* (Arthur A. Levine, 2009).

Nonfiction

Blumberg, Rhoda. *Shipwrecked!: The True Adventures of a Japanese Boy* (HarperCollins, 2001) 80p. **Japan.** **IL** 4–8 **RL** 7.2

Japan in the 1800s was unusual in many ways. For one thing, it had not been in a war for 250 years. Think about all the wars the United States has fought, and you'll realize how unusual that is. But Japan was also unusual because it did not allow any foreigners inside the country—or any Japanese out. There was actually a law that said if anyone left Japan for any reason, they could be killed if they tried to come back. The Japanese thought that foreigners were hairy, long-nosed devils, and they didn't want to be corrupted by them. (Check out the hilarious Japanese drawing of what they thought foreigners looked like on page 23.) This is the true story of a fourteen-year-old boy named Manjiro who just went out fishing (that was allowed) but was shipwrecked and trapped on an island outside of Japan. This was totally not his choice or fault, but he knew he could never go home again. He was rescued by an American whaling ship, adopted by the captain, and taken all the way to Massachusetts. He was the first Japanese person ever to set foot in the United States and was amazed at all the bizarre things he saw—glass windows, leather shoes, and chairs. Weird! But even though he was happy there, he really missed his family and wanted to go home. Japan wouldn't be so strict that it wouldn't even let a shipwrecked boy come home, would it?

Japan and Korea Book List

Since the U.S. bombing of Hiroshima and Nagasaki, Japan is now a pacifist country. Their constitution forbids them from ever declaring war against another country, and their army is only for peacekeeping purposes. But this was not always the case. This book list covers Japan's warrior history including samurai, the invasion of Korea by Japan, and battles in the Pacific during World War II.

Fiction

Goto, Scott. *The Perfect Sword* (Charlesbridge, 2008) 42p. **Japan.** IL 3–5 RL 3.7

In ancient Japan, the samurai were the warriors of the society, and creating a samurai sword was a sacred art. In this picture book, Michio, a sword-maker's apprentice, helps his master create the perfect sword. The Japanese believed that "a sword is the soul of a samurai," but whose soul is worthy of such a fine weapon? Follow Michio as he watches his master interview several samurai to test their character and values to find a master good enough to carry this perfect sword.

Kajikawa, Kimiko. *Tsunami!* Illus. Ed Young (Philomel, 2009) 32p. **Japan.** IL K–4 RL 3.3

Adapted from a nineteenth-century story, this picture book tells of a rich old man who sacrifices his own rice fields to save the villagers from a tsunami.

Park, Linda Sue. *Archer's Quest* (Clarion, 2006) 176p. **Korea.** IL 4–7 RL 3.7

A legendary archer from ancient Korea travels forward in time to twelve-year-old Kevin's bedroom in New York. Now Kevin has to find a way to get him back before he changes history forever.

Park, Linda Sue. *The Kite Fighters* (Clarion, 2000) 136p. **Korea.** IL 4–7 RL 6.3

In 1473, eleven-year-old Young-sup and his older brother Kee-sup work together to show their kite-building and -flying skills at the Korean New Year celebration.

Park, Linda Sue. *Seesaw Girl.* Illus. Jean Tseng and Mou-Sien Tseng (Clarion, 1999) 90p. **Korea.** IL 4–6 RL 5.5

An aristocratic twelve-year-old girl, Jade Blossom longs to go outside her family's walled compound in seventeenth-century Korea.

Y Park, Linda Sue. *A Single Shard* (Clarion, 2001) 192p. **Korea.** **IL** 4–7 **RL** 6.8. Newbery Medal

Tree-ear, a thirteen-year-old orphan in medieval Korea, becomes a potter's apprentice and has to prove himself to his master.

Park, Linda Sue. *When My Name Was Keoko* (Clarion, 2002) 208p. **Korea.** **IL** 5–8 **RL** 5.1

A brother and sister in Korea face the harsh Japanese occupation during World War II.

Scieszka, Jon. *Sam Samurai.* Illus. Adam McCauley (Viking, 2001) 85p. **Japan.** **IL** 2–5 **RL** 4.1

Three modern-day boys are transported to seventeenth-century Japan where they infuriate a samurai warrior.

Nonfiction

Beller, Susan Provost. *Battling in the Pacific: Soldiering in World War II* (Twenty-First Century, 2008) 112p. **Japan.** **IL** 6–9 **RL** 8.5

This book is the story of the Americans who fought World War II in the Pacific Islands against Japan.

Dean, Arlan. *Samurai: Warlords of Japan* (Children's Press, 2005) 48p. **Japan.** **IL** 4–8 **RL** 5.9

The samurai were professional warriors from the eleventh century through the nineteenth century in Japan. The leader of all the samurai was the shogun, and over time, he became even more powerful than the emperor. The samurai's main job was to fight—for honor, revenge, power, or defense. This book describes the weapons, armor, and the fighting techniques used by these valiant fighters.

Hale, Christy. *The East-West House: Noguchi's Childhood in Japan* (Lee & Low, 2009) 32p. **Japan.** **IL** 3–6 **RL** 3.6

This picture book depicts the childhood of Isamu Noguchi, a biracial boy who was shunned in Japan, but grew up to be a world-famous sculptor.

Kobayashi, Issa. *Today and Today.* Illus. G. Brian Karas (Scholastic, 2007) 32p. **Japan.** **IL** K–4 **RL** 3

Eighteen haiku by the famous Japanese poet are arranged to depict the four seasons in this picture book.

Levine, Karen. *Hana's Suitcase: A True Story* (Albert Whitman, 2003) 111p. **Japan.** **IL** 4–7 **RL** 5.2

> The suitcase of a Czech girl, Hana, who died in the Jewish Holocaust, ends up at the Tokyo Holocaust Education Resource Center and inspires the curator to learn about Hana's life.

McCully, Emily Arnold. *Manjiro: The Boy Who Risked His Life for Two Countries* (FSG, 2008) 40p. **Japan.** **IL** 3–6 **RL** 4

> In 1841 it was illegal for anyone to leave Japan. If they left and tried to come back, the punishment was death. This picture book is the true story of a fourteen-year-old fisherman who was shipwrecked, rescued by an American ship, and went to live in Massachusetts for nine years before finally going back home to Japan.

Turner, Pamela S. *Hachiko: The True Story of a Loyal Dog.* Illus. Yan Nascimbene (Houghton Mifflin, 2004) 32p. **Japan.** **IL** 1-4 **RL** 3.9

> This picture book tells the amazing true story of a dog who waited every day at the train station for his master to come home from work, and even after the master died, Hachiko still went to the station to wait every day, hoping he would come home.

Mongolia, Tibet, and Nepal Booktalks

During the ancient Mongolian Empire, Kublai Khan built his palace in what is now China. It was the last stop on the silk road, the trade route from Europe through Western Asia to China. So even though some of the content of these books takes place outside of what is now Mongolia, I chose to include them here because the Mongol heritage is so strong and fascinating, it didn't seem right to combine it with China. Likewise Tibet and Nepal. Although geographically they border China (and China has controlled Tibet's government since the 1950s), their culture and history (not to mention mountain peaks!) demand to be kept separate and recognized on their own. Kids will be excited to read these books about early explorations of Marco Polo, climbers attempting to conquer Mount Everest, and the discovery of prehistoric dinosaur eggs in the Mongol desert.

Fiction

Armstrong, Alan. *Looking for Marco Polo.* Illus. Tim Jessell (Random House, 2009) 286p. **Mongolia.** **IL** 5–7 **RL** 5.4

Mark's father is an anthropologist studying the Silk Road, the trading route that Europeans and Asians took through the Mongolian desert to get from Europe to China in the thirteenth century. The Italian Marco Polo was one of the most famous people to travel this road trading with the Mongolian emperor, Kublai Khan. When Mark's father disappears somewhere in the Gobi Desert, Mark and his mother go to Venice to see if they can contact him from the agency that funded his trip. When they get there, Mark starts to learn the stories of Marco Polo and Kublai Khan, and he learns about some of the horrifying experiences people had traveling through the desert. For example, did you know that there are flies that will attack your eyes because the moisture in them is the only water for miles? Gross. Also, Kublai Khan would kill anyone who displeased him, so Marco Polo's life was in danger all the time. He had to really watch his step! While Mark is learning all these stories, he is also having an adventure of his own exploring Venice. If you like travel stories, this one takes you practically all over the world!

Hale, Shannon. *Book of a Thousand Days* (Bloomsbury, 2007) 306p. **Mongolia.** **IL** 6–9 **RL** 5.2

This is a fantasy story based on a Brothers Grimm fairy tale called "Maid Maleen." This version takes place in medieval Mongolia, where Lady Saren's father is trying to force her to marry Lord Khasar, a vicious warrior who is a monster in more ways than one. (If you're paying attention, you'll guess his secret before the end of the book.) When Saren refuses, saying that she is already engaged to someone else named Khan Tegen, her father locks her in a tower for seven years. But she doesn't go alone. Her servant Dashti has pledged to serve her no matter what, and Dashti goes with Saren into the tower to take care of her for those seven years. While they're there, Dashti keeps a journal of their days fighting the rats in the tower, talking with Tegen who secretly comes to visit, listening as Khasar's army destroys the world outside the tower, and finally escaping. But now Dashti and Saren are completely alone, and if Khasar finds them, who knows what he will do? He is capable of anything. They have to find somewhere safe where they will be protected, but where?

Smith, Roland. *Peak* (Harcourt, 2007) 246p. **Nepal.** ⬛ 6–9 ▨ 4.5

Peak's father is a world-famous mountain climber—that's how he got the name Peak. But Peak hasn't seen his father much in the past few years since his mother remarried and they moved to New York City. That all changes when Peak gets arrested for criminal trespassing, for climbing up the outside of a skyscraper and tagging the top. The judge wants to make an example of him and send him to juvie for three years, but Peak's father shows up and offers the judge an alternative. If the judge will agree to just a fine instead of jail time, then Peak's father will take Peak to Thailand and keep him out of trouble. The judge agrees, and Peak gets on a plane. Only he's not going to Thailand. His dad has secretly arranged for Peak to join his Everest expedition. If Peak makes it, he will be the youngest person ever to reach the summit of Mount Everest. But, will he make it?

Nonfiction

Bausum, Ann. *Dragon Bones and Dinosaur Eggs: A Photobiography of Explorer Roy Chapman Andrews* (National Geographic, 2000) 64p. **Mongolia.** ⬛ 5–9 ▨ 7.9

If you've even been to the American Museum of Natural History in New York City, then you have certainly seen the huge dinosaur skeletons there. Did you ever wonder where they came from and who found them? This is the story of Roy Chapman Andrews, the first explorer to bring back dinosaur bones for the museum in the 1920s. He had a hunch that there would be fossils of ancient humans in the Mongolian desert, so he convinced the museum to send him and an exploring team on an expedition. They never did find any signs of ancient humans, but the dinosaur fossils they found sent excitement all through the scientific world. The first page of this book quotes Andrews as saying he almost died only ten times. That seems like a lot, but after reading what he had to go through on his expeditions, you'll be surprised he didn't die! This guy was like Indiana Jones, fighting snakes, bandits, and sandstorms in the desert. He definitely had an exciting life trekking through the Gobi Desert!

Greenblatt, Miriam. *Genghis Khan and the Mongol Empire* (Marshall Cavendish, 2002) 80p. **Mongolia.** ⬛ 6–8 ▨ 6.2

In the twelfth century, a ruler was born in Mongolia who would grow up to become one of the greatest military geniuses the world has ever known: Genghis Khan. The Mongols lived very different lives from how Americans live now. They lived in tents made of thick wool that protected them from the winter temperatures of twenty-five below zero. They ate meat and drank tea, but they had no vegetables because summer was too short to grow any. They wore warm fur hats and long sheepskin robes in the winter, but they believed that running water was a living spirit so they never washed their clothes. Ever. Imagine the smell! They were expert horse riders. Every child learned to ride as soon as he or she could walk. And they were expert archers. This is how Genghis Khan was able to conquer such a huge empire with his army. Their horses made them extremely mobile – they could travel really far distances much faster than anyone else could. And they were such good archers that they could shoot in any direction while galloping at full speed. This book describes how Genghis Khan built up and organized his army, and went on to conquer an enormous chunk of Asia.

Montgomery, Sy. *Saving the Ghost of the Mountain: An Expedition Among Snow Leopards in Mongolia.* Photog. Nic Bishop (Houghton Mifflin, 2009) 74p. **Mongolia.** **IL** 4–8 **RL** 5.5

In Mongolia, they call the snow leopard the "ghost of the mountain" because this mountain-dwelling creature is very rarely seen by humans. Scientists believe that there are fewer than seven thousand left in the wild. This book describes the work of Tom McCarthy, a scientist who studies them to find out how to save them from extinction. The author and photographer followed Tom on an expedition as he hiked through the mountains searching for signs of the snow leopard and gathering samples of leopard poop along the way. The book describes how, on a previous expedition, Tom was able to trap and tag a leopard with a radio collar so that he could track the leopard's movements. But even though the radio collar told them exactly where the snow leopard was, it blended into the mountains so well they still couldn't see it. Still, the snow leopard was definitely close enough to see them! At the end of this book, readers discover that none of the pictures of snow leopards were actually taken during this expedition—the author and photographer never even saw one the whole time they were there. The leopard photos are still spectacular, even if they were taken in captivity, and this book will really make you want to help save these beautiful animals.

Venables, Stephen. *To the Top: The Story of Everest* (Candlewick, 2003) 96p. **Nepal.** **IL** 4–8 **RL** 6.8

True or false: Mount Everest is named after the first person who reached the summit of the highest mountain on earth. False. Sir George Everest was not a climber; he was a mapmaker who lived in India and was fascinated by the distant Himalayas. Of course, the people who actually lived there had their own name for the mountain, Chomolungma. No human had ever been able to reach the summit alive until 1953. This book describes why it is so difficult to climb Mount Everest and how people eventually figured out how to do it. It describes the dangers of being at such high altitude without oxygen—you start to get delirious and see people who aren't there. It describes the dangers of spending the night in temperatures more than twenty degrees below zero—a disgusting picture of the author's frostbitten toes will give you a good idea. By the way, his toes were amputated after the photo was taken. It even describes how to go to bathroom when you are wearing five layers of clothing; it involves a bottle and strategically placed zippers. This book is a fascinating story about one of the most remote places in the world.

Mongolia, Tibet, and Nepal Book List

Lhasa means "land of the gods." It is the capital of Tibet and believed to be the birthplace of Tibetan Buddhism. Set in the Himalayan Mountains, it is one of the highest cities in the world, so for outsiders to get there is quite a trip! Many of the stories in this list feature the explorations of brave and curious people to one of the world's most remote places.

Fiction

Berger, Barbara Helen. *All the Way to Lhasa: A Tale from Tibet* (Philomel, 2002) 32p. Tibet. **IL** K–4 **RL** 2

In this picture book parable, a boy and his yak persevere to make the difficult journey to the holy city of Lhasa.

Michaelis, Antonia. *Dragons of Darkness.* Trans. Anthea Bell (Amulet, 2010) 568p. **Nepal. IL** 6–9 **RL** 5.3

Two boys from very different backgrounds are thrown together by magic and a common foe as they embark on a journey through the wilderness of Nepal.

Sciezska, Jon. *Marco? Polo!* Illus. Adam McCauley (Viking, 2006) 90p. **Mongolia. IL** 3–5 **RL** 2.9

Three modern-day kids are transported back in time to the court of Kublai Khan and pose as astrologers and join the caravan of Marco Polo.

Sciezska, Jon. *You Can't, but Genghis Khan.* Illus. Jennifer Frantz (HarperCollins, 2006) 80p. **Mongolia.** **IL** 2–5 **RL** 3.5

> Three modern-day kids go back to thirteenth-century Mongolia where they meet Genghis Khan.

Soros, Barbara. *Tenzin's Deer: A Tibetan Tale.* Illus. Danuta Maya (Barefoot, 2003) 32p. **Tibet.** **IL** 3–5 **RL** 3.5

> In this picture book parable, Tenzin discovers a wounded musk deer in the hills. He takes it home and heals it, but once the deer has recovered, Tenzin must let the deer go.

Nonfiction

Brown, Don. *Far Beyond the Garden Gate: Alexandra David-Neel's Journey to Lhasa* (Houghton Mifflin, 2002) 32p. **Tibet.** **IL** 3–5 **RL** 4.5

> This picture book tells the true story of the first Western woman ever to visit the Tibetan capital.

Lewin, Ted, and Betsy Lewin. *Horse Song: The Nadaam of Mongolia.* Illus. Betsy Lewin (Lee & Low, 2008) 48p. **Mongolia.** **IL** 2–6 **RL** 5.2

> Every summer, child jockeys of Mongolia gather from all over the country for an annual horse race in which they ride half-wild horses for miles across the Mongolian steppe. This travelogue takes you right into the action.

Russia Booktalks

These books only scratch the surface of understanding the largest country in the world. Reading about Princess Catherine's journey in an unheated carriage from Europe all the way across Russia, or about Napoleon's troops who walked across nine time zones to attack Russia only to be trapped there once the freezing winter set in, or about Hitler's disastrous attack on Stalingrad during World War II, you get a sense of the immense size and harshness of the country. The turbulence of the Russian Revolution is also represented here, as well as the suffering of the people under the Soviet government.

Fiction

Gregory, Kristiana. *Catherine: The Great Journey, Russia, 1743* (Scholastic, 2005) 169p. **IL** 4–7 **RL** 4.8

Fourteen-year-old Sophia lives in Prussia near Berlin, now Germany, with her family. Her mother is the niece of Prince Frederick of Sweden, and even though she married a commoner, she always hoped that Sophia would be recognized as a princess and marry into a high royal family. So she is thrilled beyond belief when Sophia gets engaged to the nephew of the Russian empress, Elizabeth. Sophia and her mother travel to Russia, where Sophia is renamed Catherine. The empress Elizabeth gives them furs and expensive jewelry, but she can also have them killed if she feels like it. Sophia tries hard to be a good princess to keep Elizabeth happy and to learn all about her new country and its people, who might one day be her subjects. Unfortunately, her mother is a greedy, conniving schemer who could ruin everything for both of them. This is a fictional diary of the real princess Catherine.

♀ Holub, Josef. *An Innocent Soldier.* Trans. Michael Hofmann (Scholastic, 2005) 231p. **IL** 6–9 **RL** 4.2. Batchelder Award

In 1812, Napoleon gathered the biggest army the world had ever seen—450,000 troops—to invade Russia. It was a disaster. The great general who was thought to be unbeatable lost three-quarters of his huge army in Russia. This is the fictional story of one boy who was conscripted into Napoleon's army. His name is Adam, and he's only sixteen, too young to join the army. But his guild master tricks him by telling the army officials that he is really his own eighteen-year-old son. The officials can tell he is too young, but they are desperate for more soldiers, so they force Adam to join. Adam becomes the servant of a lieutenant who is not much older than he is, and together they make the terrible journey across Europe into Russia. Adam's boots are too big, so his feet bleed and his toenails fall off. Men are dying of starvation because there is not enough food for all the soldiers. There isn't enough clean water either, so they have to drink from water that might have dead bodies in it. This gives them horrible diarrhea, which dehydrates them even more. And this is all before they even get to Russia! Once they start fighting, it gets unbelievably worse. The Russians have them trapped inside the country, and winter is coming. Both men and horses freeze to death, and the ones who survive eat the dead horses. Of the fifteen thousand troops in Adam's unit, only three hundred make it back alive. Adam is one of them. If you like war survival stories, you will love this book.

Whelan, Gloria. *Angel on the Square* (HarperCollins, 2001) 304p. **IL** 5–8 **RL** 6.1

In 1913 Russia, twelve-year-old Katya is thrilled to be joining her mother, a lady in waiting in the household of Tsar Nicholas II and Empress Alexandra. She has no idea that the world is in the process of huge dramatic changes that will affect her life in a big way. Her older cousin, Misha, tries to tell her of the poverty outside her sheltered life in the tsar's castle, but Katya doesn't really understand. She lives in luxury with the royal family and just assumes that everyone else is taken care of, too. But the Russian peasants are planning a revolution against the tsar and his family, and when it comes, it brings destruction to everything Katya has ever known. See also the sequel *The Impossible Journey* (HarperCollins, 2003).

Whelan, Gloria. *The Turning* (HarperCollins, 2006) 224p. **IL** 5–8 **RL** 6.1

The year is 1991 and Tatiana and Vera are preparing for a trip to Paris as dancers in the Kirov Ballet. Tatiana knows how lucky she is to be given the opportunity to go, because most people in Soviet Russia are not ever allowed to leave the country, not even for vacation. She is excited to be going but nervous too, because Vera is planning on defecting, or sneaking away, in Paris and not coming back to Russia. Defecting is illegal and dangerous. If Vera gets caught, there will be serious consequences. But life in Soviet Russia is so unfair, and they know this might be the best opportunity they have to leave. Tatiana is considering defecting herself, but she doesn't know if she wants to leave her boyfriend Sasha. And she also feels it would be wrong to abandon the other suffering people who don't have the chance to leave. But the trip is coming up soon, and Tatiana has to make a decision. What will she do? Read this book to find out.

Nonfiction

Fein, Eric. *Impossible Victory: The Battle of Stalingrad* (Capstone, 2009) 32p. **IL** 5–8 **RL** 3.5

In World War II, the German military under Hitler wanted to conquer all of Europe, and they practically did. But Hitler made a big mistake when he invaded Russia. Even though the German army was bigger (six million soldiers) and had better weapons (three thousand Panzer tanks), they still could not conquer Russia. The turning point was the Battle of Stalingrad. Of the hundreds of battles that took place during World War II, the Battle of Stalingrad was the deadliest. More than one million people were killed. What happened? How did so many people die? And why did Hitler fail?

This book tells you all the details about the weapons, the strategy, and the battle from beginning to end.

Greenblatt, Miriam. *Peter the Great and Tsarist Russia* (Marshall Cavendish, 2000) 80p. ⬛ 6–8 ⬛ 6.5

In the 1600s, Russia was a completely different place than it is now. People didn't know how to build or sail ships. Hardly anyone learned to read or write. The people wore long robes and shoes that curl up at the toes. Men never shaved their beards, or even cut them, so they were really, really long. People from other countries had to live in their own separate section of Moscow, and Russians themselves never traveled to other countries. They were so isolated they even had a separate calendar from the rest of Europe. Their calendar supposedly started at the beginning of the world, so they had no B.C.E. (Before Common Era) or C.E. (Common Era). Instead of 1698 C.E., they said the year was 7206. But the new tsar, Peter, was about to change all that. He traveled to Europe in disguise as a carpenter so that he could learn as much as he could and bring the knowledge back to Russia. He did a lot of great things, but he was also a harsh ruler. He ordered that peasants be drafted into the army for life. He more than doubled everyone's taxes. He formed a secret police force that spied on the people and tortured anyone who spoke out against him. And he built a whole new city, St. Petersburg, from the ground up. He forced laborers to work in horrible conditions where an estimated 100,000 people died. Then when no one wanted to live there, he ordered them to. Nice guy, huh? But now St. Petersburg is considered one of Peter's greatest accomplishments. So was Peter the Great really so great? Read this book and decide for yourself.

Maybarduck, Linda. *The Dancer Who Flew: A Memoir of Rudolf Nureyev.* (Tundra, 1999) 180p. ⬛ 5–8 ⬛ 6

Rudolf Nureyev was one of the most famous ballet dancers of all time. But as a child in Soviet Russia, he was poor and constantly hungry. He grew up in a cramped peasant hut shared with another family. He was miserable . . . until he started dancing. As part of his Mongolian Tatar heritage, he learned folk dancing in school. It was clear from the beginning that he was a pure, raw dancing talent. But still, his road to becoming a world-class dancer was not easy. First, his father would not let him study ballet. He wanted Rudolf to become a doctor or an engineer, but a dancer? No. By the time Rudolf finally convinced his father to let him pursue his dream, he was seventeen, and the Leningrad Ballet School said he was too old to start training. Most dancers start when they are much younger. They decided to take a chance on him and told him he would either be a "brilliant dancer—or a total failure." That just challenged Rudolf to prove them wrong. But the biggest obstacle in his life was the Communist Party in Soviet Russia. The government wanted to control everything he did, where he went, who he was friends with, everything. While on tour with the Kirov Ballet in Paris, when the Russian authorities came to escort him back to Moscow, he ran to the French police and begged to defect from Russia. He went on to become a rich and famous celebrity, but he lived in constant fear that the KGB would kidnap him and put him in prison or even kill him. This book includes lots of pictures and descriptions of Rudolf's dancing. If you are interested in ballet, you will be amazed by Rudolf Nureyev's story.

Russia Book List

Several of the books in this list focus on Russia's long history of excellence in the arts, with biographies of the painter Marc Chagall and the composer Mussorgsky.

Fiction

Celenza, Anna Harwell. *Pictures at an Exhibition.* Illus. JoAnn E. Kitchel (Charlesbridge, 2003) 32p. **IL** K–4 **RL** 3.7

Based on the true story of the Russian composer Mussorgsky, this picture book describes what inspired his famous piano suite titled *Pictures at an Exhibition.* A CD recording of the piano suite is also included with the book.

Meyer, Carolyn. *Anastasia: The Last Grand Duchess, Russia 1914* (Scholastic, 2000) 227p. **IL** 4–7 **RL** 6.4

This is the fictional diary of the last five years of Anastasia's life, spanning from royal privilege to tragedy when World War I and the Russian Revolution destroy her family.

Nonfiction

Markel, Michelle. *Dreamer from the Village: The Story of Marc Chagall.* Illus. Emily Lisker (Henry Holt, 2004) 32p. **IL** 1–4 **RL** 3

This picture book biography shows the Russian childhood of Moshe Segal, who later moved to France and became the artist Marc Chagall.

Grades 7 and Up—Fiction

Halam, Ann. *Siberia* (Random House, 2005) 262p. **IL** YA **RL** 4.3

Rosita is four years old when she and her mother arrive at the prison settlement in the middle of nowhere. She doesn't know that her mother is a political prisoner, condemned for practicing science, and soon settlement life is all she remembers. This is a dystopian science fiction story that is only metaphorically set in Siberia, where prisoners were sent after the Communist Revolution. Although there are some similarities, it is not meant to portray the actual place.

Lasky, Kathryn. *Broken Song* (Viking, 2005) 154p. **IL** YA **RL** 4.3

As a Jew in Russia in 1897, fifteen-year-old Reuven lives in fear for himself and his family as the Russian soldiers conduct pogroms (genocide) in all the Jewish villages.

Whitcomb, Laura. *The Fetch* (Houghton Mifflin, 2009) 389p. **IL** YA **RL** 5.6

If you know your Russian history, then you know that the Bolsheviks executed the Russian royal family during the Revolution in 1914. However, the bodies of the two youngest children, Anastasia and Alexei, were never found. Did they survive and escape? Or is there some other explanation? There is also a strange story about Rasputin, who was an advisor to the royal family. Legend says that he was poisoned, shot several times, and finally tied up and thrown in the river before he died. Some believe that even after all that, he still didn't die. This book is the story of Calder, a "fetch." He escorts people to the "other side" after they die, but when Calder first sees the Russian royal family, he breaks a rule of the fetch—he falls in love with a mortal. This sets off a chain of events that causes huge turmoil and some bizarre, unexplained events on earth. If you like historical fantasy, you will love this book.

Grades 7 and Up—Nonfiction

Lugovskaya, Nina. *I Want to Live: The Diary of a Young Girl in Stalin's Russia.* Trans. Andrew Bromfield (Houghton Mifflin, 2004) 280p. **IL** YA **RL** 7.1

This actual diary of a counterrevolutionary teenager who lived during Stalin's Reign of Terror shows what life was like during that time.

Western Asia Booktalks

Although we commonly call this part of the world the Middle East, I prefer to use the less Eurocentric term Western Asia, which is advocated by the United Nations. This section includes books focusing on Iraq, Iran, Afghanistan, Israel, Palestine, Kuwait, Syria, Turkey, and other countries in the Arabian peninsula. Technically, Afghanistan is considered part of Central Asia, but I have included it here because, to Americans, the conflict there seems so interrelated with Muslim extremism in the other countries in this section. Because many of these books deal with current conflicts, they are more open to controversy than the others. I have not censored books here with standpoints that people may disagree with. Rather, I encourage you to share them all with your students and start a discussion to decide if they offer a balanced view or not.

Fiction

♔ **Carmi, Daniella.** *Samir and Yonatan* (Scholastic, 2000) 186p. **Israel, Palestine.** **IL** 4–8 **RL** 5.2. Batchelder Award

Samir is a Palestinian boy living in Israeli-occupied territory. Sometimes he hears guns and explosions and knows that the Israelis are killing other Palestinians in his neighborhood or destroying their houses. His younger brother was killed by an Israeli soldier, so Samir is terrified of the soldiers. When Samir hurts his knee, he is sent to the Israeli hospital, where he shares a room with four Jewish kids. Of course, he's scared because he knows that Jews hate Palestinians, and he doesn't know what they will do to him. On top of everything, his parents can't even visit him in the hospital, because there are roadblocks that keep Palestinians out of that part of the city. But gradually, Samir realizes that they actually treat him very well at the hospital. He eats meat every day and never goes hungry like he sometimes did at home. The electricity stays on all the time, not like at home where there are often outages. And at night when everyone is asleep, his roommate, Yonatan, comes over and talks to him. Even though Yonatan is Jewish and Samir is Muslim, they become good friends, and Samir learns that deep down, all people are the same. If you like heartwarming stories about friendship overcoming prejudice, you will love this book.

♔ **Carter, Anne Laurel.** *The Shepherd's Granddaughter* (Groundwood, 2008) 224p. **Israel, Palestine.** **IL** 5–9 **RL** 3.3. Jane Addams Honor

Amani was just six years old when she knew she wanted to be a shepherd like her grandfather. So she announces that she won't go to school but she will stay home and be his apprentice. Over the years, Amani becomes really good at taking care of the sheep, helping them give birth, and protecting them from disease and danger. But things are changing, and soon she will not be able to protect them anymore. Settlers from Israel are building roads and houses right next to the sheep pastures. If they see Amani with her sheep, they will shoot, no questions asked, because they are afraid that all Palestinians are terrorists. Even though Amani's family has lived on this land for generations, the settlers are coming with the Israeli army, knocking down everything and forcing the Palestinians to leave. Amani's brother wants to fight them, but her father knows that violence is not the answer. Yet how can they convince the settlers not to take their land when the settlers won't even talk to them without guns, fences, and the army between them?

Y Ellis, Deborah. *The Breadwinner* (Douglas & McIntyre, 2001) 170p. **Afghanistan.** **IL** 4–7 **RL** 5.5. Jane Addams Honor

Parvana lives in Afghanistan with her family, but since the Taliban have taken over, her mother and her older sister have not been allowed to leave their house without wearing the burka that covers every part of them except their eyes. They are also not allowed to go anywhere without their husband, a brother, or a son to keep them company. If a woman goes out by herself or without wearing the burka, the Taliban soldiers could beat her. Parvana is only eleven years old so she doesn't have to wear the burka yet, but she is still afraid of the soldiers when she goes out with her father. One night her father is arrested for no reason and taken to prison. Besides being really sad and scared for him, the family has another problem. Without a man in the house, they can't go out to get food. They'll starve. Parvana's mother and sister have not gone outside for over a year. They're too scared of the soldiers. Parvana is the only one who can do it, but she would be safer if people thought she were a boy. So they cut her hair, and give her boy's clothes, and she goes out. Not only can she do all the family's shopping, but as a boy, she can also take over her father's business of reading and writing letters for illiterate people in the market. So Parvana becomes the breadwinner of the family while her father is in prison. But she can't pretend to be a boy forever, and what will happen if she gets caught? See also the sequels *Parvana's Journey* (Douglas & McIntyre, 2002) and *Mud City* (Douglas & McIntyre, 2003).

Tunnell, Michael O. *The Wishing Moon* (Dutton, 2004) 272p. **Iran.** **IL** 4–8 **RL** 4

You probably know the story of Aladdin and the Magic Lamp, how a genie came out of the lamp and granted him three wishes, so Aladdin became rich and married a princess and lived happily ever after. Well this book tells the story of what happens afterward. One night a homeless beggar girl, Aminah, goes to the sultan's palace to ask the princess to give her a job. Instead of having pity on the poor girl, the black-hearted wife of Aladdin looks for something to throw at her, and grabs Aladdin's ugly old brass lamp. (He never told his wife the truth about it.) So Aminah leaves with what she thinks is a worthless lamp but soon finds out there is a jinni (the Arabic spelling of genie) inside. Aminah is the new master of the lamp and can make three wishes after each full moon. Of course, she wishes for gold, and she becomes wildly wealthy and buys whatever she wants. But she keeps having nightmares about the other poor beggars still living on the streets. The only way she can stop the nightmares is by using her wishes to help other poor people. The jinni doesn't know what to make of this craziness, but he is bound to obey. So every month Aminah finds a deserving person whose life she can change with her wishes. But meanwhile, Aladdin told his wife what she had done, and she is desperate to get the lamp back at all costs. Aminah won't be able to keep it hidden from the princess' guards forever.

Nonfiction

Frank, Mitch. *Understanding the Holy Land: Answering Questions About the Israeli-Palestinian Conflict* (Viking, 2005) 152p. **Israel, Palestine.** 🔳 6–9 **RL** 9

The Jewish Israelis and Arab Palestinians have been fighting over the same piece of land for more than a century. Like, seriously fighting. You can probably turn on the news any day of the week and see some of the horrible effects this war is having on the people there. And as outside countries have taken sides in this conflict, the fight has spread all over the world. For example, because the U.S. government supports the Jews in Israel, some Arabs in several countries have formed hate groups like al-Qaeda against America. But why is this tiny piece of land so important? After all, it's only as big as New Jersey! Why can't they just share it? Or go somewhere else? How did the fight start, and why do both groups think they deserve to be the ones to control that land? This book answers all these questions, but it doesn't tell you which side is right. It just gives you the facts, and you have to decide for yourself how this problem can be solved.

O'Brien, Tony, and Mike Sullivan. *Afghan Dreams: Young Voices of Afghanistan* (Bloomsbury, 2008) 72p. **Afghanistan.** 🔳 4–9 **RL** 4

Think about every meal you have eaten this week. Now think about how much all the food you ate costs, and imagine what you would do if you had to pay for it yourself. How many hours of chores would you have to do to earn enough money? Well, that is the real situation of some of the children in this book. Many of them don't have time to go to school because they have to work to earn money. You may think you hate school, but school is easy compared to the lives of children in Afghanistan. Read this book to see what these kids, aged ten through eighteen, look like, and find out what life is like for them, how they survive, and what their hopes are for the future.

Stanley, Diane. *Saladin: Noble Prince of Islam* (HarperCollins, 2002) 48p. **Israel, Palestine.** **IL** 3–7 **RL** 5.9

In the eleventh century, Muslims lived in Jerusalem, but Christians in Europe wanted to take control of the area, so they launched the First Crusade, a war to drive the Muslims out of Jerusalem. Later, Salah-al Din was born and grew up to be a noble and wise Muslim king. Saladin heard the stories of the First Crusade and always wanted to eject the Crusaders from his land. So in 1187, his army attacked. This book describes the many years of fighting that followed until a terrifying new king of England, Richard the Lion-Hearted, joined the fight. He and Saladin finally reached a truce. If you like stories about historical battles, this picture book biography is for you.

Zwier, Lawrence J., and Matthew S. Weltig. *The Persian Gulf and Iraqi Wars: Chronicle of America's Wars* (Lerner, 2005) 96p. **Iraq, Iran, Kuwait.** **IL** 4–8 **RL** 6

You may think that the Iraq War started in 2001 with the bombing of the World Trade Center in New York City, but the conflict between the United States and Iraq had actually been brewing for a long time before that happened. This book describes the history of Iraq, from the discovery of oil in 1908 to Saddam Hussein's presidency starting in 1979. It describes how Saddam's brutal actions against neighbor country Kuwait led the first President Bush (George H. W.) to declare war against Iraq in 1991. It was called the first computer war because of all the new high-tech weapons like stealth bombers and Patriot missiles. This book tells you all about the battles and the weapons and explains the background as to why we went to war, and why we are still at war today, with Iraq. If you're into military stuff, this book describes it all.

Western Asia Book List

As the historical origin of three of the world's major religions, Judaism, Islam, and Christianity, Western Asia's history is rife with fascinating stories. Sadly, it is also rife with war. Both of these topics are represented in this book list.

Fiction

Fletcher, Susan. *Alphabet of Dreams* (Atheneum, 2006) 304p. **Iran.** ⬛ 5–8 ⬛ 4.3

In ancient Persia, Mitra and her little brother, Babak, scratch out a living by begging and stealing food, but Mitra knows they are exiled royals. Then they discover that Babak has a strange power: he can dream other people's dreams. They use this gift to gain money until they attract the attention of the wrong person.

Fletcher, Susan. *Shadow Spinner* (Atheneum, 1998) 224p. **Iran.** ⬛ 4–8 ⬛ 5.5

Every night, Shahrazad begins a story. And every morning, the sultan lets her live another day, only because he wants to hear more stories. But after one thousand nights, Shahrazad is running out of tales. Thirteen-year-old Marjan must undertake a dangerous and forbidden mission: sneak from the harem to travel the city and learn new stories for Shahrazad.

Khan, Rukhsana. *Wanting Mor* (Groundwood, 2009) 190p. **Afghanistan.** ⬛ 5–9 ⬛ 3.7

When her mother dies, Jameela's father remarries immediately and abandons Jameela in the streets of an unknown city.

LaFevers, R. L. *The Flight of the Phoenix.* Illus. Kelly Murphy (Houghton Mifflin, 2009) 256p. ⬛ 3–5 ⬛ 3.7

A young boy discovers that he is a member of a family of "beastologists" whose job it is to travel all over the world protecting rare animal species. In this book, the first of a series called <u>Nathaniel Fludd, Beastologist,</u> he travels to Arabia to save a phoenix. See also Book 2 in the series, *The Basilisk's Lair* (Houghton Mifflin, 2010).

Laird, Elizabeth. *A Little Piece of Ground* (Haymarket, 2006) 240p. **Israel, Palestine.** ⏺ 6–9 ⏺ 5

A twelve-year-old Palestinian boy tries to clear some ground for a soccer field, but living in Israeli-occupied Ramallah makes that complicated.

Mead, Alice. *Dawn and Dusk* (FSG, 2007) 152 pages. **Iran.** ⏺ 4–8 ⏺ 3.3

Thirteen-year-old Azad, a Kurdish boy living in Iran, desperately tries to cling to the life he has known, but the political situation in Iran during the war with Iraq, and Saddam Hussein's persecution of the Kurds forces his family to flee.

Nye, Naomi Shihab. *Habibi* (Simon & Schuster, 1997) 272p. **Israel, Palestine.** ⏺ 5–9 ⏺ 6.3

When fourteen-year-old Palestinian-American Liyanne and her family move to Israel, they learn firsthand about the Israeli-Palestinian conflict as they face the tensions between Jews and Palestinians.

Orlev, Uri. *The Song of the Whales.* Trans. Hillel Halkin (Houghton Mifflin, 2010) 112p. **Israel, Palestine.** ⏺ 5–8 ⏺ 6

When Michael moves to Israel, he becomes closer with his grandfather, who hands down a precious gift that allows Michael passage into his grandfather's dreams.

🏆 **Rumford, James.** *Silent Music: A Story of Baghdad* (Roaring Brook, 2008) 32p. **Iraq.** ⏺ 2–5 ⏺ 5. Jane Addams Honor

In this picture book, as bombs fall on Baghdad in 2003, a young boy practices Arabic calligraphy to distract himself from the war.

Whelan, Gloria. *Parade of Shadows* (HarperCollins, 2007) 295p. **Turkey.** ⏺ 6–9 ⏺ 6.4

In 1907, sixteen-year-old Julia goes on the adventure of a lifetime, traveling with her father from England on a tour through the desert of Turkey, experiencing romance, danger, and political intrigue.

Nonfiction

Greenwood, *Mark. The Donkey of Gallipoli: A True Story of Courage in World War I.* Illus. by Frané Lessac (Candlewick, 2008) 32 pages. Turkey. IL 3–5 **RL** 3

This picture book is based on the true story of Jack Simpson, a medic who, along with his donkey, risked his life to save wounded in soldiers in the Battle of Gallipoli in Turkey during World War I.

Nye, Naomi Shihab. *19 Varieties of Gazelle: Poems About the Middle East* (Greenwillow, 2002) 142p. **Israel, Palestine. IL** 6–9 **RL** 7.1

These new and collected poems describe Jerusalem, the West Bank, family, and being Arab-American. See also *The Flag of Childhood: Poems from the Middle East* (Aladdin, 2002).

Stamaty, Mark Alan. *Alia's Mission: Saving the Books of Iraq* (Knopf, 2004) 32p. **Iraq. IL** 3–6 **RL** 5.2

This graphic novel depicts the true story of the librarian who worked tirelessly to protect the books in her library from being destroyed in the Iraq War.

Winter, Jeanette. *The Librarian of Basra: A True Story from Iraq* (Harcourt, 2004) 32p. **Iraq. IL** 2–5 **RL** 3.4

This picture book tells the true story of a dedicated librarian who tries to rescue the books in her Basra library when war comes in 2003.

Winter, Jeanette. *Nasreen's Secret School: A True Story from Afghanistan* (Simon & Schuster, 2009) **Afghanistan. IL** 2–5 **RL** 3.4

This picture book is the true story of an Afghan girl, Nasreen, when the Taliban forbade girls to go to school. Her grandmother hears about a secret school where girls can learn, so she sends Nasreen, but if the soldiers find out, they will all be in big trouble.

Grades 7 and Up—Fiction

Jolin, Paula. *In the Name of God* (Roaring Brook, 2007) 208p. **Syria. IL** YA **RL** 4.5

Seventeen-year-old Nadia decides to become a suicide bomber in a movement aimed at supporting Muslim rule in Syria and opposing Western politics and materialism.

Kass, Pnina Moed. *Real Time* (Clarion, 2004) 186p. **Israel, Palestine.** 🔲 YA 🔲 5.3

A diverse group of teens' stories come together when they are all affected by a suicide bomb attack outside Jerusalem.

Myers, Walter Dean. *Sunrise over Fallujah* (Scholastic, 2008) 308p. **Iraq.** 🔲 YA 🔲 4.5

After graduating high school in 2003, Robin enlists in the army to help create a peaceful democracy in Iraq. But when he gets there, he finds himself in the crossfire of a very deadly war.

Zenatti, Valerie. *A Bottle in the Gaza Sea* (Bloomsbury, 2005) 149p. **Israel, Palestine.** 🔲 YA 🔲 5.8

Tal, a seventeen-year-old Israeli girl who is hopeful for peace, and an Arab Palestinian called "Gazaman" become e-mail penpals when Tal leaves a message in a bottle on the Gaza border.

Nonfiction

Ellis, Deborah. *Children of War: Voices of Iraq Refugees* (Groundwood, 2009) 128p. **Iraq.** 🔲 YA 🔲 5.2

A collection of interviews with the most tragic and innocent victims of the Iraqi War—children, many of them orphans with no access to schools, health care, clean water, or even a place to call home.

Ellis, Deborah. *Three Wishes: Palestinian and Israeli Children Speak* (Frances Lincoln, 2007) 112p. **Israel, Palestine.** 🔲 YA 🔲 4.8

Interviews with real children living through the Israeli-Palestinian conflict allow readers to see that the children caught in this conflict are just like them, but living far more difficult and dangerous lives.

Chapter 3

Europe

Ireland, Scotland, and Wales Booktalks

The overwhelming story in this section is the human rights tragedy in Ireland when the potato crop failed. A study of American immigration would not be complete without reading these books about what the Irish suffered before many came to America. But there are also happier stories about contemporary Ireland, Scotland, and Wales, as well as books that reference the ancient history, arts, music, dance, and fairy folklore that are a big part of the culture of these countries.

Fiction

Boyce, Frank Cottrell. *Framed* (HarperCollins, 2006) 320p. **Wales.** **IL** 4–8 **RL** 3.7

Dylan is the only boy in school in Manod, a small, sleepy mountain town in Wales. All of the other families with boys have moved away. There is not much for Dylan to do but record the goings-on at his family's gas station. So one day when a fancy BMW and two vans go up the mountain to the old abandoned quarry but do not come down, the whole town is wondering what they are doing up there. Because of a misunderstanding involving the Teenage Mutant Ninja Turtles, Dylan is the first to find out that the National Gallery of Art has removed all of its paintings to a secure location to protect them from flooding in London, the secure location being this tiny town. While the art is supposed to be a secret, the curator on the mountain can't resist sharing it with the people. Subsequently, it changes their lives and the town and leads Dylan and his sister to contemplate stealing one of the priceless masterpieces. Their attempt to pull off the perfect crime is botched, obviously, but readers will enjoy their scheming and plotting, wondering if they will really go through with it and if they can pull it off. *Framed* is a heartwarming and hilarious story about how art has the power to transform lives.

Higson, Charlie. *Silverfin: A James Bond Adventure* (Hyperion, 2005) 335p. Scotland. **IL** 5–8 **RL** 5.9

In a remote village in Scotland, a young boy named Alfie sneaks onto private property to go fishing—he is attacked by eels and never seen again. Meanwhile, twelve-year-old James Bond is just starting at a new school in England. He is getting used to all the rules and trying to avoid the American bully, George, who hates him. Things are going OK, but he's still really glad when Easter vacation comes and he gets to go to his aunt's home in Scotland. He hears about the missing boy Alfie and decides to do some investigating. He discovers that George's father owns an estate nearby and thinks that Alfie must have disappeared there. The more he finds out, the more he suspects that something fishy is going on—fishy, in more ways than one. If you've heard of the James Bond movies, then you know he is going to grow up to become a great secret agent, but this book imagines his adventures when he was younger. See also the other books in the James Bond Adventure series.

Parkinson, Siobhan. *Kathleen: The Celtic Knot* (American Girl, 2003) 166p. Ireland. **IL** 4–6 **RL** 5.4

Kathleen lives with her family in a tenement in Dublin, Ireland, in the 1930s. She gets teased by the girls at her Catholic school for being so poor, but she doesn't pay any attention. And when she starts taking Irish dancing lessons, she can forget all her problems and just fly! She absolutely loves dancing and quickly becomes one of the best dancers in the class. Her teacher wants her to enter in the *feis* (pronounced fesh), a competition of Irish arts. But there is one huge problem. To compete, Kathleen needs a new dancing costume, and there is no way her parents can afford one. Kathleen knows it's going to take a miracle, so she starts praying hard.

Things don't turn out exactly as Kathleen had hoped, but she still triumphs in the end. You'll admire the way she stands up to the rich girls who make fun of her. If you want inspiration for how to deal with bullies, this book is great.

Runholt, Susan. *Rescuing Seneca Crane* (Viking, 2009) 276p. **Scotland.** IL 5–8 RL 6.4

Best friends Kari and Lucas (both girls) are on vacation in Scotland with Kari's mother. They are at the Scotland Music Festival because Kari's mother is a journalist and is writing a story on Seneca Crane, a fifteen-year-old piano genius who will be performing there. So Seneca ends up spending her free time with Kari and Lucas, which is great because her mother is so strict about her music that she never gets to hang out with girls her own age. At first Kari and Lucas are in awe of Seneca because she is a professional musician, but as they get to know her, they start to feel sort of sorry for her because she doesn't have a normal life. Kari and Lucas are the first friends she's ever had. Then, after her first concert, Seneca gets kidnapped. The ransom note says not to contact the police or Seneca will be killed. Kari and Lucas have some major clues to help them find her, but can they rescue Seneca Crane without anyone getting hurt? See also *The Mystery of the Third Lucretia* (Viking, 2008).

Thompson, Kate. *The New Policeman* (Greenwillow, 2007) 441p. **Ireland.** IL 6–9 RL 4

Fifteen-year-old J.J. lives in Ireland where people don't really believe in fairies anymore, but they used to. There are old fairy rings all over the place, and some of them still have souterrains, little hidden rooms underneath where it was believed that you could cross into the fairy realm. J.J. doesn't believe that, but strange things are happening in his village. For one, it seems like time is speeding up. There is never enough time to do anything. Then J.J. hears a rumor that his great-grandfather murdered a priest, but his mother tells him the truth: the priest wasn't murdered. He disappeared without a trace. And then there is the mysterious new policeman. No one knows anything about him or where he came from. And, strangely, he can't remember why he became a policeman. He knows there is an important reason, that there is something he must do, but he doesn't remember what it is. It turns out that all of these strange things are connected, both to each other and to the fairy world. When J.J. disappears through the wall of the souterrain under the fairy ring near his house, he discovers a secret world. But can he solve the mysteries of the missing time, the missing priest, and the new policeman? And can he get back to his own world? Read this book to find out.

Giff, Patricia Reilly. *Nory Ryan's Song* (Delacorte, 2000) 148p. **Ireland.** 🔳 4–7 **RL** 4.9

Nory is twelve years old, and her family is so poor they don't always have enough money to pay the rent or buy food. Her mother is dead, and her father has been away fishing for months. He will come home soon and hopefully bring enough money for them to live. In the meantime, Nory lives with her grandfather, two sisters, and a baby brother. They have a crop of potatoes growing, so they won't starve. But one horrible day, Nory notices a rank smell coming from the potato fields. When they dig them up to look, the potatoes are all black and rotten. Over the next few months, thousands of the Irish people slowly starve to death. Nory's English landlord doesn't care that they have no food. All he cares about is collecting the rent. And if they can't pay with money, he will take their hens and their pigs, even though it's the only food they have left. Nory tries to get food any way she can, but they are running out of options. How will she survive? This book is based on the true story of the famine in 1845 when the poor Irish people starved while the rich English landlords kicked them out of their houses and sent them away. See also the sequel *Maggie's Door* (Wendy Lamb, 2003).

Newbery, Linda. *Lost Boy* (Random House, 2008) 194p. **Wales.** 🔳 4–7 **RL** 4

Matt Lanchester is riding his bike along winding roads of the Welsh village where he and his parents recently moved. He is flying down a hill when, too late, he sees an oncoming car that crashes into him head-on at full speed. Matt gets knocked off his bike onto the side of the road, and the car drives away without even stopping. After a while, Matt gets up and realizes that miraculously, none of his bones are broken. Then he looks at his bike and there isn't even a scratch. Freaky. But the freakiest thing is the cross nailed to the tree by the side of the road, with Matt's initials M.L. carved into it. Is Matt dead? If so, for how long? Or was it all just a dream? What is going on? Read this book to find out.

Nonfiction

🏆 **Bartoletti, Susan Campbell.** *Black Potatoes: The Story of the Great Irish Famine, 1845–1850* (Houghton Mifflin, 2001) 184p. **Ireland.** 🔳 6–9 🆁🅻 7.9. Sibert Medal

You might think a book about potatoes would be boring, but believe me, this book is not. You'll be hooked from the first sentence: "In 1845 a disaster struck Ireland." The potato crop failed. It doesn't sound like that much of a disaster, but for the poor people in Ireland, it was the only food they could afford, and this book goes on to describe all of the horrible things that started happening once they didn't have potatoes to eat. First, they were really hungry. There was still plenty of food in Ireland—rich people were eating all they wanted, but the poor people couldn't afford it, so many starved to death. There were riots and crime as people were desperate to get food by any means. The ones who survived often contracted diseases, really nasty ones spread by lice. Then the landlords evicted them from their homes. In some cases, they forced the evictees to sail to America or Canada whether they wanted to emigrate or not. So now this book isn't about potatoes anymore. It's about millions of starving, homeless, sick people and the injustice of rich people who watched it all happen and didn't do anything to help. If you're Irish, you should read this book and be proud and grateful that your ancestors survived this genocide.

Ireland, Scotland, and Wales Book List

Immigration stories continue in this book list, but you'll also find an eerie retelling of Macbeth, the haunted Scottish king.

Fiction

Woodruff, Elvira. *Small Beauties: The Journey of Darcy Heart O'Hara.* Illus. Adam Rex (Knopf, 2006) 32p. **Ireland.** 🔳 2–5 🆁🅻 5.2

This picture book tells a fictional story of the plight of the Irish during the potato famine from the perspective a young girl, Darcy, who watches as the landlord kicks her family out of their house and sends them on a ship to New York.

Grades 7 and Up—Fiction

Colfer, Eoin. *Airman* (Hyperion, 2008) 412p. **Ireland.** 🔳 YA 🔳 4.8

Conor Brockhart lives on the Saltee Islands off the coast of Ireland. Airplanes have not been invented yet, but Conor dreams of inventing a flying machine, until he is falsely accused of being a traitor and sent to the prison island of Little Saltee for the rest of his life . . . if he survives.

Cooney, Caroline B. *Enter Three Witches: A Story of Macbeth* (Scholastic, 2007) 281p. **Scotland.** 🔳 YA 🔳 3.9

This retelling of the Shakespeare play *Macbeth* is told from the perspective of a teenaged girl living in Macbeth's castle when the king is murdered.

Frost, Helen. *The Braid* (FSG, 2006) 95p. **Scotland.** 🔳 YA 🔳 4

Two sisters living in Scotland in the 1850s get separated when their family is forcibly evicted and deported. The older sister stays behind in Scotland and falls in love, while the younger sister starts a new life as an immigrant in Cape Breton, Canada.

Napoli, Donna Jo. *Hush: An Irish Princess' Tale* (Atheneum, 2007) 308p. **Ireland.** 🔳 YA 🔳 2.9

Melkorka is the pampered first daughter of an Irish king, but her world changes when she is kidnapped by Russian slave traders and she has to learn to deal with the brutality and harshness of her new life.

England Booktalks

London, the capital of England, is one of the largest cities in Europe, and during the Victorian era, it was the largest city in the world. The influence of English culture around the globe has been enormous, for better or worse. The books in this section reflect some of the positive effects of this influence: advances in science, trade, industry, and archaeology. They don't really reflect the negative effects of English colonization around the world. For books on that subject, please see the chapters on Africa and India.

Fiction

Dowd, Siobhan. *The London Eye Mystery* (David Fickling, 2007) 322p. **IL** 5–8 **RL** 3.4

Twelve-year-old Ted watched his cousin Salim board the London Eye, a ride like a giant ferris wheel in London that takes you way up over the city. What goes up must come down, right? Ted watched the ride, but when it came down again and the car emptied out, Salim was not in it. He disappeared without a trace. While the police are trying to find Salim, Ted and his sister Kat are doing their own investigating. Because Ted has Asperger's syndrome, it's as if his brain runs on a different operating system. Sometimes this makes people think he is freak, but other times they think he is a total genius. Can he figure out what happened to Salim? Read this book to find out.

◀ Video Booktalk: http://www.bookwink.com/archive/2010_07_18.html

LaFevers, R. L. *Theodosia and the Serpents of Chaos* (Houghton Mifflin, 2007) 343p. **IL** 4–7 **RL** 4.8

This book is dedicated to clever girls everywhere who get tired of feeling like no one's listening. That describes Theodosia perfectly. Her parents work at the British Museum of Legends and Antiquities, so Theo has learned a lot about the ancient artifacts her parents bring home from Egypt. For example, she can tell if they are cursed with black magic, and she can remove the curses, but the problem is, only she can feel the black magic and no one else believes her. When a very rare and valuable amulet called the Heart of Egypt arrives at the museum, Theo discovers that it harbors a curse so powerful that it could destroy all of England. Not only that, it is so valuable that there are dangerous criminals trying to steal it. Can Theo remove the curse and save England before the amulet falls into the wrong hands? If you like books with magic and lots of adventure, you'll love *Theodosia and the Serpents of Chaos*. See also the sequels *Theodosia and the Staff of Osiris* (Houghton Mifflin, 2008) and *Theodosia and the Eyes of Horus* (Houghton Mifflin, 2010).

◀ Video Booktalk: http://www.bookwink.com/archive_2007_07_13.html

Lawrence, Iain. *The Wreckers* (Delacorte, 1998) 196p. **IL** 5–8 **RL** 5.8

John is on a merchant ship with his father when a storm forces them to find a harbor late one night. They see some lights and think it is safe to steer their ship there, but the lights lead them straight into some jagged rocks. The ship crashes and many sailors die, but John washes onto the shore and survives. When he wakes up, he sees people walking along the beach killing the survivors. It turns out that he has washed onto the island of the Wreckers, a place where people lure ships on purpose to crash on the rocks, kill the survivors and then steal all the cargo. John is alone on this island, and he has to find out if his father is alive and get them out of there before the Wreckers find him. See also the sequels, *The Smugglers* (Delacorte, 1999) and *The Buccaneers* (Delacorte, 2001).

Video Booktalk: http://www.bookwink.com/archive_2007_09_08.html

Richards, Justin. *The Death Collector* (Bloomsbury, 2006) 336p. **IL** 5–8 **RL** 4.8

If you like historical books that are full of action and suspense and are also a little bit scary, then this is the book for you. Eddie is a young homeless orphan. He is walking alone on dark foggy London night, when he sees a dead man walking down the street. Meanwhile, at the British Museum, some thugs are trying to steal a diary donated by a famous scientist, but they botch the job and end up accidentally killing the museum's curator. Eddie doesn't know it yet, but these two events are related, and he is about to become mixed up in the sinister plot of a brilliant but evil scientist who wants to control the world by creating an army of the living dead. This book is a nonstop action filled page-turner. You won't want to put it down.

Video Booktalk: http://www.bookwink.com/archive_2007_01_15.html

Skelton, Matthew. *Endymion Spring* (Delacorte, 2006) 392p. **IL** 4–7 **RL** 7.1

This book shifts between the fifteenth-century laboratory of Johannes Gutenberg and the twenty-first-century library at Oxford University in England. Gutenberg's apprentice, Endymion Spring, discovers an ancient and secret form of writing that has the potential to reveal all knowledge. However, he must run for his life to escape the evil Johann Fust who wants to use this knowledge for his own sinister ends. Six centuries later, in the shelves of the Oxford Library, twelve-year-old Blake finds an old book with a cryptic riddle that only he can read. He and his sister realize that they have stumbled upon the rare and valuable book of Endymion Spring. Now their lives are in danger as well because of the modern-day scholars who have been searching and waiting for years to get their hands on the book. If you want a book with fantasy, history, and modern suspense, this book has it all!

Springer, Nancy. *The Case of the Missing Marquess: An Enola Holmes Mystery* (Philomel, 2006) 208p. **IL** 4–8 **RL** 7.1

On Enola Holmes's fourteenth birthday, her mother leaves her a present, and then goes out—but doesn't return. Ever. What could have happened to her? Worried, Enola contacts her older brothers, Mycroft and Sherlock Holmes, in London and asks them to come home and try to piece together the puzzle. They think Enola is just a stupid girl, and they want to send her to boarding school to get her out of the way. But you know Sherlock Holmes's little sister must have some detective skills, and she realizes that the clues to her mother's whereabouts are in the birthday present she left for Enola. Unlocking the clues sends Enola on a wild and dangerous chase across Victorian England to find her mother. See also other books in the Enola Holmes Mystery series.

Williams, Marcia. *Archie's War* (Candlewick, 2007) 46p. **IL** 4–6 **RL** 4.3

This is the scrapbook of a ten-year-old boy named Archie. At first it's just a regular scrapbook with family pictures and cartoons that he draws to depict his life. But when his uncle leaves to go fight in the Great War in 1914, the scrapbook becomes a collection of letters, postcards, and news clippings about World War I, both in the trenches in Germany and at home in England. The cool thing about this book is that the letters open up so you really feel like you're reading an actual letter in someone's scrapbook.

Nonfiction

♈ **Dash, Joan.** *The Longitude Prize.* Illus. Dusan Petricic (FSG, 2000) 200p. **IL** 6–9 **RL** 8.7. Sibert Honor

In the eighteenth century, it was dangerous for sailors to travel long distances because they had no way of knowing where they were at sea. They could measure latitude, that is, how far north or south they were from the Equator, but they had no way to measure longitude, how far east or west they had traveled. To get from Europe to North America, they just traveled along straight lines, kind of like ocean highways so they wouldn't get lost. The problem with this was it made it too easy for pirates to attack them. All they had to do was wait for a ship to show up, and they could attack it. So finally the British Parliament decided to do something about it. They offered a prize of 20,000 pounds (the equivalent of $12 million today!) to the first person who could come up with an accurate way to measure longitude at sea. Of course, scholars and well-known scientists all tried fancy theories, but they couldn't do it. An uneducated carpenter named John Harrison had his own idea. The earth rotates fifteen degrees each hour, so if you had a clock that could tell you exactly how long you have been traveling, then you would know exactly how many degrees you've covered. No clocks existed with that kind of accuracy yet, and certainly not at sea, but John Harrison spent half his life building one. And he did it! He solved the longitude problem! But the snooty scholars on the prize committee dismissed him as an uneducated tinkerer. They refused to believe that his clock would work. Would he ever get the recognition and the prize money he deserved?

Steele, Philip. *Isaac Newton: The Scientist Who Changed Everything* (National Geographic, 2007) 64p. ■ IL 4–8 ■ RL 8.3

Isaac Newton was born in Lincolnshire, England, the son of a respectable farmer, but as he grew up, it was clear that he had no interest in farming. He wanted to go to college, so in 1661, he enrolled at Cambridge University, one of the best schools in England, which still exists today. He became fascinated with math and science, but then the bubonic plague hit London, and they had to send all the students home. While at home, Isaac conducted his own experiments. He developed algebra theories and invented a new kind of math called calculus. He did some dangerous experiments with light (looking into the sun, and poking a needle behind his eyeball—do NOT try this at home!). But the work for which he is best known is his theories about gravity, supposedly inspired by watching an apple fall from a tree in his yard. He theorized that gravity is the force that keeps us from flying off the earth. It's also the force that keeps the moon and planets from flying off into space or from crashing down onto earth. He spent the next twenty years finalizing his theories about gravity into what we now call Newton's Laws of Motion. They held true for three hundred years, and without them space travel would never have been possible. Up until the twentieth century, no one was able to challenge Newton's Laws of Motion, and the first person who could was the genius Albert Einstein.

England Book List

You'll find a lot of historical territory covered in the books that follow, from medieval England to contemporary England, and even England of the future.

Fiction

🏆 **Avi.** *Crispin: The Cross of Lead* (Hyperion, 2002) 262p. **IL** 4–7 **RL** 6.1.
Newbery Medal

Falsely accused of theft and murder, an orphaned peasant boy in
fourteenth-century England flees his village and eventually discovers the
truth about his parents. See also the sequel, *Crispin: At the Edge of the
World* (Hyperion, 2006) and *Crispin: The End of Time* (Balzer + Bray,
2010).

Blackwood, Gary. *The Shakespeare Stealer* (Dutton, 1998) 216p. **IL** 4–7 **RL**
5.5

Shakespeare's plays were wildly popular even in his own time, so it's
easy to believe that Widge's master would want him to steal Shakespeare's
newest play, *Hamlet.* But when Widge becomes friends with Shakespeare
and everyone at the Globe Theater, he refuses to steal from them. See also
the sequels *Shakespeare's Scribe* (Dutton, 2000) and *Shakespeare's Spy*
(Dutton, 2003).

Boyce, Frank Cottrell. *Cosmic* (Walden Pond, 2010) 320p. **IL** 4–8 **RL** 4.2

Liam is only twelve-years-old, but his size makes people think he is an
adult. He tries to see how far this can take him and ends up on a rocket ship
in space.

Boyce, Frank Cottrell. *Millions* (HarperCollins, 2005) 272p. **IL** 4–8 **RL** 6.9

A fourth-grade boy finds millions worth of stolen money and thinks
it's a gift from God, so he starts giving it all away. But his older brother has
other ideas, and of course the actual robbers want their money back, too.

Cushman, Karen. *Alchemy and Meggy Swann* (Clarion, 2010) 176p. **IL** 4–7 **RL** 6

In this novel of Elizabethan England, Meggy is sent to London to live
with her alchemist father whom she has never known.

Gardner, Sally. *I, Coriander* (Dial, 2005) 280p. **IL** 4–8 **RL** 5.2

In seventeenth-century London, Coriander, a girl who has inherited
magic from her mother, must find a way to use it to save herself and an
inhabitant of the fairy world where her mother was born.

Harrison, Michelle. *13 Treasures* (Little, Brown, 2010) 368p. ▊ 4–7 ▊ 5

Thirteen-year-old Tanya's insistence that she can see fairies gets her banished to her grandmother's secluded countryside manor, where she finds herself entangled in a mystery that could trap her in the fairy realm forever.

Ibbotson, Eva. *Dial-a-Ghost.* Illus. Kevin Hawkes (Dutton, 2001) 195p. ▊ 4–7 ▊ 5.7

A family of friendly ghosts protects a British orphan from the evil plans of his greedy guardians.

Ibbotson, Eva. *The Dragonfly Pool.* Illus. Kevin Hawkes (Dutton, 2008) 377p. ▊ 4–7 ▊ 6.4

Tally is miserable about having to go away to boarding school, but when she gets there, she finds it is wonderful beyond all her hopes.

McKay, Hillary. *Wishing for Tomorrow: The Sequel to "A Little Princess."* Illus. Nick Maland (Margaret K. McElderry, 2010) 288p. ▊ 4–7 ▊ 5.3

This new sequel to Frances Hodgson Burnett's classic sends Sarah Crewe and her maid Becky away to the country, leaving the other girls behind at Miss Minchin's.

Meyer, Carolyn. *Patience, Princess Catherine* (Harcourt, 2004) 198p. ▊ 6–9 ▊ 7.4

Catherine of Aragon leaves her home and her family to marry Arthur, the prince of England, but when Arthur suddenly dies, her future becomes very unclear. See also the other books in the Young Royals series, *Doomed Queen Anne* (Harcourt, 2002), *Beware, Princess Elizabeth* (Harcourt, 2001), and *Mary, Bloody Mary* (Harcourt, 1999).

♟ **Schlitz, Laura Amy.** *Good Masters! Sweet Ladies! Voices from a Medieval Village* (Candlewick, 2007) 85p. ▊ 5–8 ▊ 7.6. Newbery Medal

Different characters, between ten and fifteen years old, who live in or near a thirteenth-century English manor describe their lives in short monologues.

Skelton, Matthew. *The Story of Cirrus Flux* (Delacorte, 2010). 304p. ▊ 4–7 ▊ 5.5

In a steampunk alternate eighteenth-century London, twelve-year-old orphan Cirrus Flux becomes mixed up with the mysterious "Guild" because of a magical substance his father may have collected.

Wood, Maryrose. *The Incorrigible Children of Ashton Place: The Mysterious Howling.* Illus. Jon Klassen (Balzer + Bray, 2010) 267p. **IL** 3–6 **RL** 8.5

When Miss Lumley arrives at Ashton Place to be the governess to three foundling children, she has no idea what she is in for—these children were raised by wolves! Literally!

Woodruff, Elvira. *Fearless* (Scholastic, 2008) 222p. **IL** 4–7 **RL** 4.8

An orphan becomes the apprentice to an eccentric inventor but faces his worst nightmare when a storm threatens the Cornwall coast where they live.

Woodruff, Elvira. *The Ravenmaster's Secret: Escape from the Tower of London* (Scholastic, 2003) 225p. **IL** 4–7 **RL** 4.9

In eighteenth-century London, the eleven-year-old son of the Ravenmaster, who lives in the prison tower, befriends the daughter of a Jacobite rebel who is being held prisoner there.

Nonfiction

Adams, Simon. *Elizabeth I: The Outcast Who Became England's Queen* (National Geographic, 2005) 64p. **IL** 4–8 **RL** 7

This biography of Henry VIII's daughter, Princess Elizabeth, describes the turmoil her father caused in her life by marrying and then divorcing or executing six women (including her mother) and changing the national religion of England from Catholicism to Protestantism. Through it all, Elizabeth I survived to eventually become queen.

Aronson, Marc. *If Stones Could Speak: Unlocking the Secrets of Stonehenge* (National Geographic, 2010) 64p. **IL** 4–7 **RL** 9.6

This book examines the archaeological clues to the origins and purpose of Stonehenge.

Bond, Rebecca. *In the Belly of an Ox: The Unexpected Photographic Adventures of Richard and Cherry Kearton* (Houghton Mifflin, 2009) 32p. **IL** 2–5 **RL** 7.5

This picture book describes the lives of two brothers who found ingenious ways to photograph bird nests in the nineteenth-century English countryside.

Lasky, Kathryn. *The Man Who Made Time Travel.* Illus. Kevin Hawkes (FSG, 2003) 42p. **IL** 4–6 **RL** 4.9

This picture book describes the lifelong quest of John Harrison to create a clock that would accurately measure longitude at sea.

Grades 7 and Up—Fiction

Crowley, Suzanne. *The Stolen One* (Greenwillow, 2009) 416p. **IL** YA **RL** 5.5

Sixteen-year-old Kat goes to London to find answers about her real parents, and she ends up being invited into Queen Elizabeth's court. This book is based on a true sixteenth-century mystery.

Dowswell, Peter. *Powder Monkey: Adventures of a Young Sailor* (Bloomsbury, 2005) 276p. **IL** YA **RL** 6

Thirteen-year-old Sam thought it would a great adventure to go to sea and work on a merchant ship. But when the British Royal Navy boards the ship and forces Sam to join them, he realizes how harsh, grueling, and dangerous a life at sea is for a navy man. See also the sequels *Prison Ship* (Bloomsbury, 2006) and *Battle Fleet* (Bloomsbury, 2008).

Gray, Keith. *Ostrich Boys* (Random House, 2010) 304p. **IL** YA **RL** 4.5

When their best friend dies in an accident, three boys steal his ashes and take them on a road trip to Scotland.

Lawrence, Iain. *The Convicts* (2005) 208p. **IL** 6–9 **RL** 5.2

When his father lands in debtors' prison, fourteen-year-old Tom tries to survive on the rough streets of early-nineteenth-century London. See also the sequels *The Cannibals* (Delacorte, 2005) and *The Castaways* (Delacorte, 2007).

Lloyd, Saci. *The Carbon Diaries 2015* (Holiday House, 2008) 330p. **IL** YA **RL** 3.7

Sixteen-year-old Laura describes the chaos that ensues when England imposes radical carbon dioxide rationing to combat climate change. See also the sequel *The Carbon Diaries 2017* (Holiday House, 2010).

Reeve, Philip. *Here Lies Arthur* (Scholastic, 2008) **IL** YA **RL** 5.6

When Gwynna's village is burned, she runs away to hide from the invading soldiers, but the old bard Myrddin finds her and uses her to stage some pretend magic to convince the soldiers to accept Arthur as their king.

Reeve, Philip. *Mortal Engines* (HarperCollins, 2003) 310p. **IL** YA **RL** 6.8

In the distant future, a fifteen-year-old apprentice is forced out of London and must survive in the perilous Out-Country. See also the sequels *Predator's Gold* (Eos, 2004), *Infernal Devices* (Eos, 2006), *A Darkling Plain* (HarperCollins, 2007) and the prequel *Fever Crumb* (Scholastic, 2010).

♈Rennison, Louise. *Angus, Thongs and Full-Frontal Snogging* (HarperTeen, 2001) 272p. **IL** YA **RL** 5.7. Printz Honor

Fourteen-year-old Georgia writes in her diary about the hilarious happenings in her life. See also the other books in the Confessions of Georgia Nicolson series.

Turnbull, Ann. *No Shame, No Fear* (Candlewick, 2004) 293p. **IL** YA **RL** 5.9

In seventeenth-century England, Susanna, a young Quaker servant girl, falls in love with seventeen-year-old Will, an apprentice from a wealthy family. With Quakers being persecuted and imprisoned, can their bond survive, no matter what?

Grades 7 and Up—Nonfiction

♈Heiligman, Deborah. *Charles and Emma: The Darwins' Leap of Faith* (Henry Holt, 2009) 268p. **IL** YA **RL** 7.1. Printz Honor

Charles Darwin wrote his theory of evolution knowing that it would upset many Christians, including his own beloved wife. This biography describes the personal struggle he had at home to reconcile his theory with the opposition he knew it would receive.

France, Spain, and Switzerland Booktalks

Between D-Day, the trenches of World War I, and the Nazi invasion of Paris, the French have had their share of wars fought in their country. Despite that (or maybe because of it?), France now receives the most foreign tourists of any country in the world. Even for students not planning a trip to France, reading about past wars makes an exciting study of the country, especially for boys. Books about Spain and Switzerland are much less represented here. In fact, there is only one book set in Switzerland, *Unfinished Angel* by Sharon Creech.

Fiction

Creech, Sharon. *Unfinished Angel* (HarperCollins, 2009) 164p. **Switzerland.** ▪️
4–7 ▪️ 5.3

An angel lives in the Swiss Alps and watches over the people in the village, but it's an unfinished angel and it's not sure it's doing it right—or what it is really supposed to be doing at all. It floats and swishes around and "flishes" calming thoughts into people's minds and occasionally pinches them when they do bad things, but it doesn't really know what its purpose is . . . until Zola moves in. Most people can't see Angel, so it is very surprised when Zola recognizes it right away and starts bossing it around! She tells Angel about a group of homeless orphans living in the village and asks what it is going to do about them. This is "shockful" and "tragical" to Angel, but when it tries to help the children, it ends up causing even more trouble in the village. Can this funny bungling unfinished angel figure out how to take care of all the "peoples" in his village? This book may remind some readers of *The BFG* by Roald Dahl. If you like funny books with a heartwarming message, then you'll love this one.

Lindo, Elvira. *Manolito Four Eyes.* Illus. Emilio Urberuaga, Trans. Joanne Moriarty (Marshall Cavendish, 2008) 144p. **Spain.** ▪️ 3–6 ▪️ 5.8

Ten-year-old Manolito lives in Madrid, Spain. There are a couple of things you should know about Manolito. One is that most people know him by his nickname "Four-Eyes" because he has worn glasses since he was five and because all the cool kids have nicknames. The second thing is that this kid is hilarious! He makes everything that happens to him seem funny, like going out with his disastrous first girlfriend "the One-and-Only Susannah" until she dumps him for Ozzy, the biggest bully in school and probably in all of Spain. Or the time he dressed as a penguin to represent World Peace. Or the time he and his grandfather almost got mugged . . . which doesn't sound funny, but it was because Manolito is a true original. There is no one like him in the "worldwide world." See also the sequels *Manolito Four-Eyes: The 2nd Volume of the Great Encyclopedia of My Life* (Marshall Cavendish, 2009) and *Manolito Four-Eyes: The 3rd Volume of the Great Encyclopedia of My Life* (Marshal Cavendish, 2010).

Myers, Walter Dean. *The Journal of Scott Pendleton Collins: A World War II Soldier* (Scholastic, 1999) 144p. **France.** ▪️ 6–9 ▪️ 5.3

By 1944, the Germans had taken over France, but the British and American armies had a plan for taking it back, the Normandy Invasion on D-Day, June 6. They sailed across the English Channel to Normandy,

France, but when they got there, the Germans were ready for them, all lined up on the beach with guns. As soon as the sailors stepped off the boats, they were shot at, and many were killed before they even reached the shore. This is a fictional diary of one soldier who survived. Even though it's fictional, this book is so realistic, you feel like you are there at the battle.

◀ Video Booktalk: http://www.bookwink.com/archive_2006_10_18.html

Riordan, Rick. *The 39 Clues: The Maze of Bones* (Scholastic, 2008) 220p. **France.** **IL** 4–7 **RL** 3.3

Amy and Dan Cahill's parents died when they were young. They know their grandmother, Grace Cahill, is wealthy and that they have rich relatives all over the world. But when Grace dies and those relatives are summoned for the reading of her will, Amy and Dan get a shock. It turns out that the Cahills are descendents of the world's most powerful family in history. The secret to their power is a mystery, but the person who can discover it will become the richest, most powerful person in the world. In Grace's will, she gives everyone a choice: join a dangerous search for 39 clues that will reveal the secret of the Cahill family power or take $1 million and walk away. Amy and Dan make their choice and join a deadly race that takes them to Paris to find clues that will unlock the secret of human power over the centuries. This book is a nonstop action ride! See also the other books in the 39 Clues series.

Nonfiction

Borden, Louise. *The Journey That Saved Curious George: The True Wartime Escape of Margret and H.A. Rey.* Illus. Allan Drummond (Houghton Mifflin, 2005) 72p. **France.** **IL** 4–8 **RL** 6.4

You have probably all heard of the children's book character Curious George, the mischievous little monkey who always got into trouble and had to be saved by the Man in the Yellow Hat. But you probably don't know that the original manuscript for the story had an adventure of its own during World War II and traveled with its author on a harrowing escape from the Nazis in France. The author, Hans Reyersbach, was living in Paris with his wife, Margret, when the German army invaded. On a rainy morning in June 1940, Hans and his wife packed up their most precious belongings, only what they could carry in baskets on their bicycles, and fled south from the city. Included in Hans's basket was the unpublished manuscript for his first children's book, which would later become *Curious George*. This book describes the history of Curious George and his author, their long journey through France, and their safe arrival in New York.

Desaix, Deborah Durland, and Karen Gray Ruelle. *Hidden on the Mountain: Stories of Children Sheltered from the Nazis in Le Chambon* (Holiday House, 2007) 275p. **France.** ■ 6–9 ■ 5

During World War II, the Nazis took over France, and it was not safe for Jews anywhere in the country. But there were many people who hid the Jews and protected them from the Nazis. This is the true story of a town in the French Alps that sheltered several thousand Jewish children. The people of the town were Huguenot Protestant and had been persecuted themselves in France, so when they heard about the persecution of the Jews, the church ministers acted quickly to set up children's homes. The people also opened their own homes, and it is said that almost every farm on the mountain was hiding at least one Jewish refugee. It was dangerous work, and one of the ministers was even sent to prison, but that didn't stop them. This book includes pictures and interviews from people who were sheltered in the mountain town of Le Chambon.

McClafferty, Carla Killough. *Something Out of Nothing: Marie Curie and Radium* (FSG, 2006) 134p. **France.** ■ 5–8 ■ 6.8

In 1903, Polish-born Marie Curie became the first woman to win a Nobel Prize. She won with her husband Pierre for their work researching radioactivity and discovering the element radium. Even though they were famous, they were never rich because they gave away all their research. In fact, Marie was so grateful to her adoptive country that during World War I, she volunteered to set up mobile x-ray labs for the soldiers all over France. Marie and her husband were constantly working and constantly sick, but they didn't know it was because of the radium they were exposed to day in and day out. No one knew then how dangerous it was to touch radioactive elements. In fact, once doctors found that they could use radium to destroy cancer cells, people thought radium was a miracle cure for everything. They actually drank it as a tonic in their water! But they didn't realize that the radium was destroying other cells, too. This book describes the life and work of an amazing scientist, but it also describes how the discovery of radiation changed the world, for better and worse.

Murphy, Jim. *Truce: The Day the Soldiers Stopped Fighting* (Scholastic, 2009) 116p. **France.** ■ 5–9 ■ 12.6

In 1914, Austria-Hungary attacked Serbia, and one by one, the military powers of Europe all chose sides and started fighting "The Great War," what we now call World War I. But this war was different from any previous war because the twentieth-century weapons were much more destructive than anything soldiers ever experienced before. Machine guns and heavy artillery were new and enormously lethal weapons, especially because the soldiers did not have any protective gear, not even helmets. Worse still, the war never had to happen at all. It only started because Germany told Austria-Hungary to attack, but at the last minute, Germany changed its mind, but it was too late. The war had already started, and there was no backing down. So the German army advanced into France, where it was met by the British army. Each side dug trenches where they could fire at the other side and then hide. The trenches were disgusting and miserable places to live, with rain, mud, and dead bodies everywhere. Plus, there was the constant fear of being killed. Anyone who left the trench to go "over the top" risked being seen and shot at by the enemy. But on Christmas Eve 1914, a miraculous thing happened. The Germans in their trenches lit Christmas trees and started singing "Silent Night." The British in their trenches listened and then sang their own carols. On Christmas morning they woke up to absolute silence, no guns at all, and that day, both sides unofficially agreed to a truce. Some even went over the top to meet and celebrate Christmas with the enemy soldiers. This book shows actual photographs the soldiers took of each other during that day. It was only a temporary truce, but it is still an amazing story.

France and Spain Book List

The predominant theme of the books in this list continues to be World War II in France, but you will also find other aspects of French history represented, as well as some biographies of famous Spanish figures, Antoni Gaudi and Federico Garcia Lorca.

Fiction

♆ **Goscinny, René.** *Nicholas*. Illus. Jean-Jacques Sempé. Trans. Anthea Bell (Phaidon, 2005) 126p. **France.** **IL** 4–7 **RL** 6.3. Batchelder Honor
This new translation introduces American readers to the hilarious escapades of Nicholas and his classmates at an all-boys school in France. See also the other books in the <u>Nicholas</u> series.

Gregory, Kristiana. *Eleanor, Crown Jewel of Aquitaine* (Scholastic, 2002) 187p. **France.** **IL** 4–7 **RL** 5.9
The fictional twelfth-century diary of Eleanor, who became queen of France at age fifteen.

Maltbie, P. I. *Picasso and Minou.* Illus. Pau Estrada (Charlesbridge, 2005) 32p. **France.** 🆔 K-4 🆁🆛 3.9

This picture book is based on a true story of the artist Picasso, who lived in poverty in Paris during his "Blue Period," and his amazing cat named Minou.

McCaughrean, Geraldine. *The Death-Defying Pepper Roux* (HarperCollins, 2009) 328p. **France.** 🆔 6–9 🆁🆛 6.4

Pepper Roux's aunt prophesied that he would die before he was fourteen, so when he wakes up on his fourteenth birthday still alive, he doesn't know what went wrong, but he runs away pretending to be different people hoping that death won't find him and realize the mistake.

🏆 **Morgenstern, Susie. Secret Letters from 0–10.** Trans. Gill Rosner (Viking, 1998) 137p. **France.** 🆔 4–7 🆁🆛 6.1. Batchelder Honor

Ten-year-old Ernest lives a boring, predictable existence in Paris with his grandmother until a new girl at school shakes up his life. See also the Batchelder Honor-winning *The Book of Coupons* (Viking, 2001).

🏆 **Mourlevat, Jean-Claude.** *The Pull of the Ocean.* Trans. Y. Maudet (Delacorte, 2006) 190p. **France.** 🆔 6–9 🆁🆛 3.3. Batchelder Award

In this modern retelling of "Tom Thumb," seven brothers in modern-day France run away from home, led by the youngest who, although mute and unusually small, is exceptionally wise.

Rappaport, Doreen. *The Secret Seder.* Illus. Emily Arnold McCully (Hyperion, 2003) 32p. **France.** 🆔 2–5 🆁🆛 3

This picture book depicts a night during the Nazi occupation of France, when a boy and his father sneak out to join a group of fellow Jews at a seder.

Scott, Elaine. *Secrets of the Cirque Medrano* (Charlesbridge, 2008) 216p. **France.** 🆔 4–7 🆁🆛 4.3

In the Paris village of Montmartre in 1904, fourteen-year-old Brigitte works in her aunt's café, where she serves the colorful customers, such as Russian revolutionaries, circus performers, and the artist Pablo Picasso, who frequent it.

♟ **Selznick, Brian.** *The Invention of Hugo Cabret* (Scholastic, 2006) 544p. **France.** 🔲 4–7 🔲 4.8. Caldecott Medal

An orphan living secretly in the walls of the Paris train station works to repair an automaton that he thinks may have a message from his dead father. Pictures and text tell the story in this amazing picture book/novel.

Nonfiction

Drez, Ronald J. *Remember D-Day: The Plan, the Invasion, the Horror Stories* (National Geographic, 2004) 61p. **France.** 🔲 4–8 🔲 7

This book discusses the events and personalities involved in the momentous Allied invasion of France on June 6, 1944.

♟ **Lázaro, Georgina.** *Federico García Lorca.* Illus. Enrique S. Moreiro (Lectorum, 2009) 32p. **Spain.** 🔲 4–6. Pura Belpré Honor

This is a picture book biography written in Spanish verse about twentieth-century poet and playwright Federico García Lorca.

Rodriguez, Rachel. *Building on Nature: The Life of Antoni Gaudi.* Illus. Julie Paschkis (Henry Holt, 2009) 32p. **Spain.** 🔲 1–4 🔲 2.2

This picture book biography of the famous Catalonian architect highlights his imagination and originality and will inspire readers to see the buildings he created.

Ruelle, Karen Gray, and Deborah Durland DeSaix. *The Grand Mosque of Paris: How the Muslims Rescued Jews During the Holocaust* (Holiday House, 2009) 40p. **France.** 🔲 4–6 🔲 11.3

This picture book tells the true story of a Muslim mosque in the center of Nazi-controlled Paris that helped shelter Jews during World War II.

Grades 7 and Up—Fiction

Elliot, L. M. *Under a War-Torn Sky* (Hyperion, 2001) 284p. **France.** 🔲 YA 🔲 6.4

After his plane is shot down in German-occupied France, nineteen-year-old Henry Forester of Richmond, Virginia, must walk across the country in hopes of rejoining his unit. See also the sequel, *A Troubled Peace* (Katherine Tegen, 2009).

Gardner, Sally. *The Red Necklace* (Dial, 2007) 378p. **France. IL** YA **RL** 4.8

When the evil Count Kalliovsky murders his master, Yann must run for his life to escape him, but the French Revolution is brewing, and everything is about to change. See also the sequel, *The Silver Blade* (Dial, 2009).

Grant, K. M. *Blue Flame* (Walker, 2008) 246p. **France, Spain. IL** YA **RL** 5.6

This book takes place in 1242 in Occitania, a small region between France and Spain, and tells of the escalating conflict between Catholics and Cathars. See also the other books in the Perfect Fire Trilogy.

Jablonski, Carla. *Resistance: Book 1.* Illus. Leland Purvis (First Second, 2010) 128p. **France. IL** YA

The first of a trilogy, this graphic novel tells the story of kids in Nazi-occupied France who work in the underground resistance.

Meyer, Carolyn. *Marie, Dancing* (Harcourt, 2005) 260p. **France. IL** YA **RL** 6.1

A fictionalized autobiography of Marie Van Goethem, a poor ballerina who became the model for Edgar Degas's famous sculpture, "The Little Dancer."

Mosher, Richard. *Zazoo* (Clarion, 2001) 224p. **France. RL** 6.5

A thirteen-year-old Vietnamese orphan raised in rural France by her aging "Grand-Pierre" falls in love for the first time and discovers old family secrets from World War II.

Nonfiction

McClafferty, Carla Killough. *In Defiance of Hitler: The Secret Mission of Varian Fry* (FSG, 2008) 196p. **France. IL** YA **RL** 6.8

A biography of Varian Fry, an American who went to France to help rescue Jews and others who were wanted by the Nazis, by smuggling them out of the country.

Italy Booktalks

During ancient Roman times, Italy was the center of Western civilization, and Rome is still the country's capital, although of a much smaller republic. Books about ancient Rome are not included here because they have their own section in the chapter on Ancient Civilizations. During the fourteenth century, Italian influence expanded again as the Renaissance started there, spreading new modern ideas throughout Europe.

Fiction

Armstrong, Alan. *Looking for Marco Polo.* Illus. Tim Jessell (Random House, 2009) 286p. **IL** 4–7 **RL** 5.4

Mark's father is an anthropologist studying the Silk Road, the trading route that Europeans and Asians took through the Mongolian desert to get from Europe to China in the thirteenth century. The Italian Marco Polo was one of the most famous people to travel this road trading with the Mongolian emperor Kublai Khan. When Mark's father disappears somewhere in the Gobi Desert, Mark and his mother go to Venice to see if they can contact him from the agency that funded his trip. When they get there, Mark starts to learn the stories of Marco Polo and Kublai Khan, and he learns about some of the horrifying experiences people had traveling through the desert. For example, did you know that there are flies that will attack your eyes because the moisture in them is the only water for miles? Gross. Also, Khan would kill anyone who displeased him, so Marco Polo's life was in danger all the time. He had to really watch his step! While Mark is learning all these stories, he is also having an adventure of his own exploring Venice. So if you like travel stories, this one takes you practically all over the world!

Avi. *Murder at Midnight* (Scholastic, 2009) 254p. **IL** 4–7 **RL** 3.3

Orphan boy Fabrizio is the servant to a great magician named Mangus. Fabrizio really tries to be a good servant because he doesn't want to end up on the streets, but the problem is, he's a bumbling fool and drives Mangus crazy. When Mangus is accused of using magic to help overthrow the king, poor Fabrizio is determined to help him. But can he help save his master, or will his babbling and stumbling efforts just make things worse? If you like mystery and adventure with a little bit of humor too, you will love this book. See also *Midnight Magic* (Scholastic, 1999).

Baccalario, P. D. *Ring of Fire.* Illus. Iacopo Bruno. Trans. Leah D. Janeczko (Random House, 2009) 293p. **IL** 5–8 **RL** 3.8

On a snowy night in Rome, four kids, all strangers from different countries, end up sleeping in the same room in an overbooked hotel. Strangely enough, they find out they all have the same birthday. But what seems at first like innocent chance is really fate at work, bringing them together for a very important mission. That night, they meet a man who begs them to take his briefcase and keep it safe. They do, and the next day they find out that he was murdered soon after. Why? What is in that briefcase that is so valuable that someone would kill for it? Who was after that man, and what will the ruthless killer do when he traces it back to the kids? The kids figure out that the briefcase holds the clues to finding the Ring of Fire, an ancient object with incredible power, and they *must* find it before it's too late. This book is fast-paced and exciting, but I have to warn you, there are some scary parts, and one *really* scary part that you might want to skip if you don't like blood (page 263). See also the other books in the Century Quartet.

Barnhouse, Rebecca. *The Book of the Maidservant* (Random House, 2009) 232p. **IL** 4–7 **RL** 5.3

In the Middle Ages, religious Christians went on pilgrimages to various places to see holy relics of the Christian saints and martyrs. This book is based on the true story of one of the most famous medieval pilgrims, Margery Kempe. Only the story is told by her servant, Johanna, and Johanna does not think her mistress Margery is so saintly. In fact, her mistress is downright irritating. Margery cries at the suffering of the Virgin Mary and prays at the top of her lungs; she preaches at everyone and tells them that they are not holy enough, while at the same time telling Johanna to cook for her and do her laundry. But Johanna stays by her because without her mistress, she knows she will never make it back home to England. Once in Italy, though, they are separated, and Johanna is alone in a strange country where she has no home, no food, and no money, and she can't speak the language. How will she survive one week, much less make it back to England?

♀ Bjork, Cristina. *Vendela in Venice.* Illus. Inga-Karin Eriksson. Trans. Patricia Crampton (R&S Books, 1999) 93p. **IL** 3–5 **RL** 5.4. Batchelder Honor

Imagine a city with no cars, no buses, and no lawns, just water everywhere. That's what Venice, Italy, is really like. The houses are built on top of stilts with steps leading out of the water right up to the front door. Instead of driving on roads, people travel by boat in the canals. This is the story of a Swedish girl named Vendela who visits Venice for the first time. You see the city through her eyes: the canals, the gondolas, the museums, the art, the architecture, and the food. Reading this book will show you why Venice is called a fairy-tale city, and it will totally make you want to go there!

♀ Funke, Cornelia. *The Thief Lord.* Trans. Oliver Latsch (Scholastic, 2001) 349p. **IL** 4–7 **RL** 4.9. Batchelder Honor

Orphaned brothers Prosper and Bo have run away from their aunt who wants to separate them. They fall in with a gang of homeless street kids in Venice who are led by a boy named the Thief Lord. Meanwhile, the aunt hires a detective to track down the kids and return them. If the detective uncovers their hiding place, then all the kids will be in danger. But they are in danger already because the Thief Lord has accepted a job stealing a mysterious broken wooden wing from a fancy house in town. If the kids get caught, there will be huge trouble, but what actually happens is even more bizarre than anyone expected.

Napoli, Donna Jo. *Stones in Water* (Dutton, 1997) 209p. **IL** 4–8 **RL** 6.5

This is a fictional story based on events that actually happened in Italy during World War II. Thirteen-year-old Roberto was at the movies with his friends when all of a sudden, Nazi soldiers came and rounded up all the boys and forced them onto trains all the way to Germany. The boys became slaves and were forced to work under horrible conditions in the German work camps. But the worst part is that Roberto's best friend Samuel is Jewish, and if the Nazis find out, they'll kill them both. Can Roberto and Samuel escape the work camp and get back to Italy? Read this book to find out. See also the sequel *Fire in the Hills* (Dutton, 2006).

🎬 Video Booktalk: http://www.bookwink.com/archive_2006_10_18.html

Nonfiction

Byrd, Robert. *Leonardo: Beautiful Dreamer* (Dutton, 2003) 48p. **IL** 3–7 **RL** 5.9

Sometimes when you ask little kids what they want to be when they grow up, they tell you like ten different things. "I want to be a fireman and a baseball player and an artist and a pilot and a chef and a doctor and . . . ." You get the idea. Well, I don't know what Leonardo wanted to be when he was a young boy in Vinci, Italy, but he ended up doing at least ten different things when he grew up. And he did them all so well that kings hired him and he is still famous today—more than five hundred years later. First he was a painter. You have probably heard of one of his most famous paintings, the *Mona Lisa*. But he was also a sculptor, an inventor, a scientist, a mathematician, an astronomer, an architect, a theater director, an engineer, a costume designer, and a musician. Another interesting fact about Leonardo is that his notebooks have no organization whatsoever—all his random thoughts and ideas are just jumbled in there wherever they can fit. Not only that, but he wrote them upside down and backward, so the writing only looks normal if you hold it up to a mirror. No one knows why he did it. Maybe it's because he was left-handed. You lefties out there, do you do that, too? Is that a lefty thing? Read this book to find out more of the strange and amazing things he did in his life. And when your teachers complain about your messy notebook, you can say that you're like Leonardo da Vinci, legendary genius!

Fritz, Jean. *Leonardo's Horse.* Illus. Hudson Talbot (G. P. Putnam's Sons, 2001) 48p. **IL** 3-6 **RL** 4.1

The great Leonardo da Vinci lived in an exciting place during an exciting time. The Renaissance was exploding with interest in art and new ideas. He was commissioned to create a bronze statue of a horse for the duke of Milan. So he went and studied the movements of horses. He created sketches and a model for the sculpture, but he had so many other projects going on, like painting *The Last Supper* and the *Mona Lisa* and trying to build a flying machine, that he never actually completed the horse sculpture. Hundreds of years later in 1977, a man named Charlie Dent read about the unfinished horse and decided to finish it for Leonardo. This is the true story of how Italy finally got its bronze horse statue.

Steele, Philip. *Galileo: The Genius Who Faced the Inquisition* (National Geographic, 2005) 64p. **IL** 4–8 **RL** 6

What would you do if you knew something was true beyond any doubt, but no one believed you? Would you still try to convince people that you were right, even if they arrested you and put you on trial? Or would you just give up and let them think they are right? Well that's what happened to Galileo. Today everyone now knows that Earth and the other planets revolve around the sun, but when Galileo was born in Italy in 1564, people believed that the sun revolved around the earth. This book describes Galileo's childhood, his college years studying mathematics, and his invention of the telescope. With the telescope, he was able to see things that no one had ever seen before: the surface of the moon, other planets in our solar system, and moons orbiting those other planets. These observations led Galileo to the certainty that the Earth was revolving around the sun, but he knew he could get in serious trouble for saying that—arrested for sure and maybe even put to death. Read this book to find out what he decided to do.

Italy Book List

If you didn't know that Italy was basically the center of the world during the Renaissance from the fourteenth through sixteenth centuries, these books should give you a clue that there was something exciting going on then. You'll find more books here about the geniuses Michelangelo, Leonardo, and Galileo.

Fiction

Grey, Christopher. *Leonardo's Shadow: Or My Astonishing Life as Leonardo da Vinci's Servant* (Atheneum, 2006) 390p. **IL** 6–9 **RL** 4.8

Fifteen-year-old Giacomo, servant to Leonardo da Vinci, helps his procrastinating master finish painting *The Last Supper* while trying to discover who his real parents are in fifteenth-century Milan, Italy.

Macdonald, Wendy. *Galileo's Leaning Tower Experiment: A Science Adventure.* Illus. Paolo Rui (Charlesbridge, 2009) 32p. **IL** K–4 **RL** 2.9

This picture book illustrates the story of how Galileo tested his theories about gravity by dropping objects from the Leaning Tower of Pisa.

Marsden, Carolyn. *Take Me with You* (Candlewick, 2010) 176p. **IL** 4–7 **RL** 3.7

Two girls have grown up as best friends in a Catholic orphanage. While they hope to be adopted someday, they dread the possibility of being separated.

Meyer, Carolyn. *Duchessina: A Novel of Catherine de Medici* (Harcourt, 2007) 197p. **IL** 6–9 **RL** 11

The noble young Italian Catherine de Medici is raised in convents. In 1533, when she is fourteen, she becomes engaged to Prince Henri of France, who is destined to become king.

Napoli, Donna Jo. *Daughter of Venice* (Wendy Lamb, 2002) 275p. **IL** 4–7 **RL** 4.9

In sixteenth-century Venice, fourteen-year-old Donata, disguised as a boy, sneaks out of her noble family's house to explore the world outside her sheltered life.

Napoli, Donna Jo. *The Smile* (Dutton, 2008) 272p. **IL** 6–9 **RL** 3

On a visit to Florence, thirteen-year-old Elisabetta catches the eye of the great Leonardo da Vinci and falls for a boy named Giuliano de Medici, but it is a dangerous time for the Medicis. As tragedy and chaos threaten their happiness, *Mona Lisa* faces the bittersweet truth of love.

Napoli, Donna Jo. *Three Days* (Dutton, 2001) 151p. **IL** 4–7 **RL** 4.6

Eleven-year-old Jackie is stranded alone in Italy when her father suddenly dies while driving on the highway.

Scieszka, Jon. *Da Wild, Da Crazy, Da Vinci.* Illus. Adam McCauley (Viking, 2004) 96p. **IL** 3–5 **RL** 3.7

Three modern-day kids are transported back in time to sixteenth-century Italy where they meet Leonardo da Vinci.

Shefelman, Janice. *Anna Maria's Gift.* Illus. Robert Papp (Random House, 2010) 104p. **IL** 3–5 **RL** 3

When her father dies, nine-year-old Anna Maria goes to Venice to live at an orphanage and becomes a violin student of the great composer Vivaldi.

Nonfiction

D'Agnese, Joseph. *Blockhead: The Life of Fibonacci.* Illus. John O'Brien (Henry Holt, 2010) 40p. **IL** 2-5 **RL** 2.3

While much is not known about the great thirteenth-century mathematician's life, this picture book biography explains his famous theories.

Stanley, Diane. *Michelangelo* (HarperCollins, 2000) 48p. **IL** 4–7 **RL** 5.9

A biography of the brilliant artist from Florence who actually dissected dead bodies to understand how to make his sculptures more lifelike. (Warning: this book contains a kind of creepy illustration of him dissecting a dead body.)

Grades 7 and Up—Fiction

Peterfreund, Diana. *Rampant* (HarperTeen, 2009) 402p. **IL** YA **RL** 4.5

Astrid thinks her mother is crazy for believing they are descendents of a long line of unicorn hunters, but when a unicorn attacks Astrid's boyfriend, she is forced to change her mind. Now that there seems to be a resurgence of them, she travels to a cloisters in Rome to study the old techniques of unicorn hunting. See also the sequel *Ascendant* (HarperCollins, 2010).

Grades 7 and Up—Nonfiction

Krull, Kathleen. *Leonardo da Vinci.* Illus. Boris Kulikov (Penguin Viking, 2005) 124p. **IL** YA **RL** 6.2

This biography of the great artist and inventor describes how his illegitimate birth and presumed homosexuality may have allowed him (or forced him) to expand his thinking beyond the boundaries of middle-class Italian society.

Germany, The Netherlands, and Austria Booktalks

Because the Nazi Party was born in Germany, it would be hard to ignore books about World War II and the Jewish Holocaust here. These books explore the effects Nazi power had on German civilians and Jews. Obviously, Jews suffered much more, but these books also show the effects on Germany after the war, with the partition of Germany into East and West. For more books dealing with the victims of the Jewish Holocaust, see also the section on Eastern Europe.

Fiction

Bartoletti, Susan Campbell. *The Boy Who Dared* (Scholastic, 2008) 192p. Germany. **IL** 6–9 **RL** 4.3

This story is fiction but it is based on a real person, Helmut Hubener, a sixteen-year-old German boy who was executed for treason against the Nazi Party. This book starts with him in his jail cell waiting for the executioner to come and end his life. The rest of the story is told in flashbacks that show Helmut's childhood. When he was young, he admired the Nazis, and he wanted to be a soldier for the Fatherland, Germany. But as he grew up, he began to see the ways that Hitler's government was unfair. Germans were not allowed to read non-German books. They couldn't listen to non-German radio stations. If they dared to say anything negative about Hitler or the government, they were severely punished, tortured, and sent to concentration camps and prison. Helmut was one boy who dared to speak the truth that he saw, and he was killed for it.

Fleming, Candace. *Boxes for Katje.* Illus. Stacey Dresses-McQueen (FSG, 2003) 36p. **The Netherlands.** **IL** K–4 **RL** 2.3

In Europe right after World War II, many people were starving. They barely had enough food or clothing. Everything they had was lost, stolen, or ruined during the war. When Americans heard about this, they started sending boxes of needed things to the people. They sent food, clothes, and special treats. This picture book is based on the true story of the author's mother, who sent a box to Holland. When Katje receives the box, she is so grateful that she sends a letter back. And then another box comes. And then another. Katje shares everything with the people in her town, and they are all so grateful that they want to send something back to their friends in America. But what can they send? Katje thinks of the perfect thing. There are still wars going on around the world right now. Maybe you can find a way to send a box to a child in another country.

Ibbotson, Eva. *The Star of Kazan.* Illus. Kevin Hawkes (Dutton, 2004) 416p. **Austria.** **IL** 4–7 **RL** 5.6

Eleven-year-old Annika was abandoned as a baby. She was found by two kind old women, who brought her home and cared for her. She is happy there, but she always dreams of a day when her real mother will come back for her. In her imagination, Annika's real mother is rich, beautiful, and glamorous. So when one day, a rich, beautiful, and glamorous woman shows up and claims to be her mother, Annika doesn't think twice. She leaves her old life behind and goes to live with the mystery woman in her castle. But her life there is much worse than Annika thought it would be. It turns out that her so-called mother is not as kind or as rich as Annika thought, and she is desperate to get her hands on Annika's Star of Kazan necklace. Will Annika be able to escape her cruel, conniving mother and go back to the family that loves her?

◄ Video Booktalk: http://www.bookwink.com/archive_2007_01_15.html

Schroder, Monika. *The Dog in the Wood* (Front Street, 2009) 163p. **Germany.** **IL** 4–7 **RL** 4.4

It's 1945 and Fritz lives with his family on their farm in the eastern part of Germany. His father died fighting for the Nazis. Germany is losing the war, but Fritz's grandfather, the Nazi leader in the village, refuses to surrender to the Russian troops whose tanks are rolling into Germany. Then the news comes that Hitler is dead and the Russians will be there within days, and Fritz's grandfather kills himself. So Fritz's mother puts a white flag of surrender on their house and offers to give the soldiers whatever they want, food, even her house to stay in so the soldiers won't hurt them. At first they are more or less peaceful, but with the end of the war, changes are coming to eastern Germany. The Russians installed a Communist government, and they want to punish the Nazis and take away their land. So they tell Fritz's mother that her property is too big and will be divided and given away to other farmers. The whole family has to leave right away. But where will they go, and how will they live? Fritz's father and grandfather were Nazis, but Fritz never hurt anyone—he's only ten years old! This story is fiction but is based on true stories of life in Germany after the war.

Whelan, Gloria. *After the Train* (HarperCollins, 2009) 152p. **Germany.** **IL** 4–7 **RL** 5.2

Imagine finding out the people who you thought were your parents are not, and you are not who you always thought you were. That's what happens to Peter in this book. He lives in West Germany. World War II has been over for ten years, and he wishes people would just stop talking about it. But then he finds out the secret his parents have been hiding from him since the war. Now all of a sudden, Peter wants to find out everything that happened then, and find out more about who he *really* is.

Nonfiction

Metselaar, Menno, and Ruud van der Rol. *Anne Frank: Her Life in Words and Pictures from the Archives of the Anne Frank House.* Trans. Arnold J. Pomerans (Roaring Brook, 2009) 215p. **The Netherlands.** **IL** 4–9 **RL** 6

Anne Frank was a Jewish teenager who hid from the Nazis in Amsterdam for two years before being caught and sent to die in a concentration camp. She is famous now because her diary from this time period survives so we can read about what her life was like, what she thought, felt, and experienced. There are lots of versions of the diary out there, but this book is cool because it is like holding Anne's actual diary from the 1940s. It shows photos of the cover and the inside pages in her own handwriting. You can see where she pasted in pictures of herself and her family. It also shows what her life was like in the concentration camp after she stopped writing her diary. (Warning: there is one disturbing picture of British soldiers carrying corpses away for burial.) Reading her diary and looking at the pictures of Anne with her family is so heartbreaking for many readers because they really feel as though they know and like this girl. She was so friendly, happy, and interesting. Not only that, she was so normal. Even though she has to live in a cramped apartment where she has to be completely silent and can't ever go outside, she writes about things that any girl can relate to: how her mother gets on her nerves, how she is falling in love with another boy who's hiding there, and how she wishes everyone would just stop criticizing her and let her be herself. Reading this book may make you think that if you had known her, you would totally have wanted to be her friend.

Germany, The Netherlands, and Austria Book List

There are more books here about the Jewish Holocaust, but you will also find books about Holland's history of painting and tulip mania, as well as a steampunk fantasy set in an alternate Austria during World War I (*Leviathan* by Scott Westerfeld).

Fiction

Dahlberg, Maurine F. *Escape to West Berlin* (FSG, 2004) 179p. **Germany.** 🔲 4–7 **RL** 5.1

In 1961 East Berlin, thirteen-year-old Heidi copes with normal teenage stress plus the threat of separation from West Berlin if the border closes.

Glatshteyn, Yankev. *Emil and Karl.* Trans. Jeffrey Shandler (Roaring Brook, 2006) 194p. **Austria.** 🔲 4–7 **RL** 3.9

In Vienna, Austria, two nine-year-old boys become orphans when the Nazis take their parents. This book was originally written in 1940 and fictionalizes the chaos that existed during that time in Europe.

Lasky, Kathryn. *Ashes* (Viking, 2010) 320p. **Germany.** ▆ 6–9 ▆ 4.7

Thirteen-year-old Gabriella's favorite pastime is reading, but when the Nazis gain power, she fears she may have to give up the life and the books she has always cherished.

Noyes, Deborah. *Hana in the Time of the Tulips.* Illus. Bagram Ibatoulline (Candlewick, 2004) 32p. **The Netherlands.** ▆ 2–5 ▆ 4

A picture book of what life was like for a little girl during the tulipomania craze in seventeenth-century Holland.

Westerfeld, Scott. *Leviathan.* Illus. Keith Thompson (Simon Pulse, 2009) 440p. **Austria.** ▆ 6–9 ▆ 5.2

Set in a fictional alternate universe, this steampunk fantasy describes World War I from the perspective of Aleksander Ferdinand, prince of the Austro-Hungarian Empire.

Nonfiction

Engle, Maragarita. *Summer Birds: The Butterflies of Maria Merian.* Illus. Julie Paschkis (Henry Holt, 2010) 32p. **Germany.** ▆ K–4 ▆ 4

This picture book biography tells the story of the seventeenth-century naturalist who discovered that butterflies hatch from cocoons, disproving religious superstitions about them.

♈ Judge, Lita. *One Thousand Tracings: Healing the Wounds of World War II* (Hyperion 2007) 40p. **Germany.** ▆ 3–5 ▆ 4.3. Jane Addams Honor

This picture book describes the relief effort of a mother and daughter in America who aided numerous German families after World War II.

Levy, Debbie. *The Year of Goodbyes: A True Story of Friendship, Family and Farewells* (Hyperion, 2010) 144p. **Germany.** ▆ 4–7 ▆ 5

Excerpts from the 1938 poetry album that the author's mother kept as an eleven-year old while waiting for a visa to leave Germany.

♈ McCann, Michelle R. *Luba: The Angel of Bergen-Belsen.* Illus. Ann Marshall (Tricycle, 2003) 45p. **Germany.** ▆ 3–5 ▆ 4.3. Jane Addams Honor

This picture book biography tells the amazing true story of Luba Tryszynska, a prisoner at a German concentration camp who hid and protected fifty-four children from being killed by Nazi soldiers.

Rubin, Susan Goldman. *The Anne Frank Case: Simon Wiesenthal's Search for the Truth.* Illus. Bill Farnsworth (Holiday House, 2009) 40p. **Austria.** 🔲 4–7 **RL** 5.9

A picture book biography of a famous Jewish Holocaust survivor Simon Wiesenthal, who worked to prove to Holocaust deniers that it was in fact real.

Grades 7 and Up—Fiction

🏆 **Chotjewitz, David.** *Daniel Half-Human and the Good Nazi.* Trans. Doris Orgel (Atheneum, 2004) 298p. **Germany.** 🔲 YA **RL** 5.6. Batchelder Honor

In 1933, best friends Daniel and Armin admire Hitler, but when Daniel learns he is half Jewish, their friendship changes, just as life in Hamburg is changing all around them.

🏆 **Zusack, Marcus.** *The Book Thief* (Knopf, 2006) 560p. **Germany.** 🔲 YA **RL** 4. Printz Honor

For her own protection, Liesel is sent away from her mother to a foster home outside of Munich during World War II. With the help of her foster father, she learns to read and copes with the war and the injustices of the Nazis.

Grades 7 and Up—Nonfiction

🏆 **Bartoletti, Susan Campbell.** *Hitler Youth: Growing Up in Hitler's Shadow* (Scholastic, 2004) 176p. **Germany.** 🔲 YA **RL** 7.8. Newbery Honor, Sibert Honor

Based on first-person accounts, this book tells the true stories of several young people growing up in Germany during the Nazi regime.

🏆 **Giblin, James Cross.** *The Life and Death of Adolf Hitler* (Clarion, 2002) 246p. **Germany.** 🔲 YA **RL** 8.1. Sibert Medal

This biography delves into the life of the terrible dictator and shows how he rose to his position of power. It describes the important people and events in his life and reveals some interesting facts. For example, Hitler was a vegetarian. This book explains why he never ate meat!

Scandinavia and Iceland Booktalks

Scandinavia includes Norway, Sweden, Denmark, and Finland. Norway is called the Land of the Midnight Sun because in summer, parts of the country have twenty hours of daylight (but in the winter, there are only four hours of daylight). Vikings, trolls, and beserker warriors all figure prominently in the books in this section. Many of them are fantasies that don't name the specific country where they are set, but if they were inspired by Norse legends or lore, I listed them as books about Norway, even though, strictly speaking, they are not. World War II also had an impact on Scandinavia, where the people are very proud of their resistance to the Nazis and their large-scale successful effort to protect as many Jews as they could. With so much focus on German aggression during World War II, it is easy to overlook Russia's invasion of Finland, but it is an interesting war story, especially because it is rare to find books where the Allied forces are the aggressors.

Fiction

Durbin, William. *Winter War* (Random House, 2008) 231p. **Finland.** 🆄 6–9 🆁🅻 4

In 1809, Russia conquered Finland and stayed there until 1917 when Finland declared its independence. But in the winter of 1939, Russia invaded again, and that is where this fictional story begins. Marko's world changes one day when the Russians bomb his town, and his best friend is killed. Marko had polio a few years before, and his left leg was damaged. He limps when he walks, but he can still ski just fine, even with his leg brace. In the Finland winter, skiing is the best way to get around. So Marko decides to join the army, not as a soldier—he is too young—but as a ski messenger. His job is to ski from camp to camp, sometimes in temperatures way below zero, delivering messages to the Finnish officers. It is incredibly tiring and incredibly dangerous, but just as Marko never gave up when the doctors told him he wouldn't walk again, he's not going to give up now when his country needs him. If you like exciting war stories, you will love this book.

Farmer, Nancy. *The Sea of Trolls* (Atheneum, 2004) 459p. **Norway.** 🆄 4–7 🆁🅻 6.2

In the year 793, Jack is the bard's apprentice and is learning how to do magic. When their village is attacked by Viking raiders (called beserkers because they are so crazy and fearless in battle), Jack and his master try to protect the village. But Jack and his sister end up getting kidnapped by the Viking chief, Olaf. They are taken away as slaves on his ship to Ivar the Boneless, a horribly cruel king who rules in the savage kingdom of trolls. See also the sequels, *The Land of the Silver Apples* (Atheneum, 2007), and *The Islands of the Blessed* (Atheneum, 2009).

George, Jessica Day. *Sun and Moon, Ice and Snow* (Bloomsbury, 2008) 328p. **Norway.** **IL** 6–9 **RL** 4.8

When the pika was born, her mother was so disappointed at having another girl that she couldn't even be bothered to give her a name, so her eight brothers and sisters just called her the pika, which means girl. Her mother wanted a boy to bring wealth and fame to the family; all girls are good for is cooking and cleaning. But the pika is special. She has the ability to speak to animals and understand what they are saying. This ability allows her to help her family with the farm animals, but one cruel night, her gift changes their lives forever when an enchanted polar bear barges into their home and asks the pika to come live with him in his palace for one year. He says he won't harm her, but he needs her to come and can't say why. She agrees to go if the bear will make her family rich while she's gone. If you know the story of Beauty and the Beast, you have some idea of what happens next, but this book goes into a lot more detail about pika's life in the palace and her desperate fight with the evil witch who wants pika to fail.

Langrish, Katherine. *Troll Fell* (HarperCollins, 2004) 355p. **Norway.** **IL** 4–7 **RL** 4

Peer's father has just died, and Peer is an orphan with no family left—or so he thinks, until a horrible, brutish man named Baldur shows up claiming to be his uncle. It turns out that Peer's father ran away from his cruel stepfather when he was younger, and Baldur is one of the cruel stepfather's sons. So Peer finds out that he has two uncles, and he has to go live with them no matter how awful they are. Family is family. Baldur takes Peer to his new home in Troll Fell, a bleak, spooky place where trolls and other magical creatures come out at night. Peer is miserable. His uncles make him sleep in the barn. They treat him like a servant and barely give him or his dog any food. He does make a few friends; one is an equally miserable magical creature called Nis, who tells him secrets about the trolls. Another is Hilde, a girl his age whose family hates Peer's uncles as much as he does. But when Peer discovers the real reason his uncles brought him to Troll Fell, he realizes that he and his friends are in great danger. The greedy uncles need a pair of humans to sell to the trolls in exchange for gold. Peer has to find a way to stop them, or he and Hilde will both become troll slaves forever. If you like books with magic and adventure, you will love *Troll Fell.* See also the sequels *Troll Mill* (HarperCollins, 2006) and *Troll Blood* (HarperCollins, 2008).

Y **Thor, Annika.** *A Faraway Island.* Trans. Linda Schenck (Delacorte, 2009) 247p. **Sweden.** IL 4–7 RL 4.2. Batchelder Award

Imagine there was a war going on in your country and it was too dangerous for you to stay there, but your parents weren't allowed to leave. Would you want them to send you alone with your younger sister to another country to live with another family and learn another language? Even if it might save your life, would you want to be separated from your parents, not knowing when or if you would ever see them again? That is exactly what happens to Stephie and Nellie in this book. Their parents arrange for them to leave Nazi-controlled Austria to go live in Sweden while their parents try to get permission to move to the United States. Stephie and Nellie have to deal with the usual difficulties of moving to a new place—finding their way around, making new friends, dealing with bullies—but on top of that, they have to learn a new language, new customs, and get used to a new set of parents! It's not easy. This book is based on a true story. In 1939, families in Sweden took in Jewish children to protect them from the Nazis. Sadly, adults were not allowed to come too, and many of the children never saw their parents again.

Nonfiction

Berger, Melvin, and Gilda Berger. *The Real Vikings: Craftsmen, Traders and Fearsome Raiders* (National Geographic, 2003) 55p. **Norway, Sweden, Denmark.** IL 4–7 RL 6

When you think of Vikings, you think of wild warriors with those huge battle axes and swords, or you think of those enormous wooden boats with the curved up ends, or you think of a blond woman with braids and a hat with horns sticking out. This is all true (except for the horns in the hat; that image is from an opera, not real history), but the Vikings were more than just savage raiders. They were fearless explorers, expert crafters, and they even started one of the earliest democratic governments. This book tells the real story about the Vikings—how the cold and darkness in Norway, Denmark, and Sweden made survival so difficult that many Scandinavians left to explore the world and trade with other countries. People now think they even made it as far as New York, way before Columbus was born. Of course, they did also conquer large parts of

England, so their reputation as fierce killers is deserved, but this book gives you the whole story.

Levine, Ellen. *Darkness over Denmark: The Danish Resistance and the Rescue of Jews* (Holiday House, 2000) 164p. **Denmark.** ⬛ 5–8 ⬛ 7.2

When Nazi soldiers came and occupied Denmark during World War II, the Danes didn't try to fight. There were only 4 million of them against 75 million Germans; they knew they could never win, so the Danish government agreed to cooperate with the German Nazis. But they refused to let them change their laws or their Danish way of life. For centuries, the Danish people believed that all Danes should be free to practice any religion. In other Nazi-occupied countries like Poland and Czechoslovakia, soldiers were rounding up all the Jews and sending them away either to ghettos or concentration camps, but the Danish government made the Nazis promise not to do this. Most Danes hated the Nazis and hated that they were occupying their country, so they formed secret resistance groups that would do small acts of sabotage. They would slash tires of German military vehicles and blow up German factories. But when the Nazis broke their promise about not touching Danish Jews, all the Danish citizens joined together to secretly hide and transport as many Jews to safety as they could. Almost all of the eight thousand Jews in Denmark were saved. They were the only country in Europe that was able to ruin Hitler's plan. How did they do it? Read this amazing true story to find out.

Nardo, Don. *Tycho Brahe: Pioneer of Astronomy* (Compass Point, 2008) 111p. **Denmark.** ⬛ 5–7 ⬛ 7

Imagine that you were really into astronomy and you knew the positions of every star in the sky. Then imagine that one night you saw a new star, brighter than all the others, that you know was not there before. This happened to Tycho Brahe (pronounced TEE-ko BRA-hee) in Denmark in 1572, and it freaked him out. In those days, people believed that God had made all the stars and planets, and they all revolved around Earth in the same, unchangeable way forever. A new star was just not possible. So Tycho studied the star every night, measured its distance from Earth, and mapped its movements in the sky. Then one night, it disappeared. We now suspect it was a supernova that burned out, but Tycho had no idea what happened. He did know that the old way of thinking about the stars being unchangeable was incorrect. So he spent his life trying to figure out what was really going on, and he became a legend in his own time, both for his research and for his eccentric ways. It is said that he wore a metal nose because his real nose was cut off in a sword fight. Even though he was a little strange, and even though the theory he came up with to describe the movement of stars and planets was wrong, his research still helped moved science forward.

Scandinavia and Iceland Book List

Although it is 600 miles from Norway, Iceland is sometimes considered a Scandinavian country, and it shares Scandinavia's Norse heritage. So books about Iceland are included in this list.

Fiction

Y Bredsdorff, Bodil. *The Crow-Girl: The Children of Crow Cove.* Trans. Faith Ingwersen (FSG, 2004). 160p. **Denmark.** **IL** 4–6 **RL** 5.4. Batchelder Honor

> After her grandmother dies, a young orphaned girl leaves her house by the cove and begins a journey alone to make a new life for herself. See also the Batchelder Honor–winning sequel, *Eidi* (FSG, 2009).

Deedy, Carmen Agra. *The Yellow Star: The Legend of King Christian X of Denmark.* Illus. Henri Sorenson (Peachtree, 2000) 32p. **Denmark.** **IL** 2–5 **RL** 3.5

> This picture book tells the story of King Christian X and the Danish resistance to the Nazis during World War II.

Gaiman, Neil. *Odd and the Frost Giants.* Illus. Brett Helquist (HarperCollins, 2009) 117p. **Norway.** **IL** 4–6 **RL** 5.4

> Odd meets three talking animals who are really the Norse gods who have been tricked by a frost giant. They need Odd's help to go to Asgard and get the frost giant to change them back.

Pattou, Edith. *East* (Harcourt, 2003) 498p. **Norway.** **IL** 6–9 **RL** 6.4

> In this retelling of the Scandinavian folktale "East of the Sun, West of the Moon," Rose agrees to be taken away by a great white bear in exchange for helping her family. The bear takes her to an enchanted castle where she realizes too late that he is suffering under a cruel witch's spell and only she can save him.

Scieszka, Jon. *Viking It and Liking It.* Illus. Adam McCauley (Viking, 2002) 73p. **Norway, Sweden, Denmark.** 🔲 3–5 🔲 4.1

> Three modern-day kids are transported back in time to the Viking era.

Toksvig, Sandi. *Hitler's Canary* (Roaring Brook, 2007) 192p. **Denmark.** 🔲 4–7 🔲 4.8

> Based on the true story of the Danish Resistance to the Nazis in 1940, this book details how Bamse and his brother join the Resistance and help rescue Jews from being taken to concentration camps.

Nonfiction

McMillan, Bruce. *Going Fishing* (Houghton Mifflin, 2005) 32p. **Iceland.** 🔲 1–4 🔲 2.8

> This is a photo-documentary of a young Icelandic boy fishing with his grandfathers. See also *Nights of the Pufflings* (Houghton Mifflin, 1995), *My Horse of the North* (Scholastic, 1997), and *Days of the Ducklings* (Houghton Mifflin, 2001).

Grades 7 and Up—Fiction

Cadnum, Michael. *Daughter of the Wind* (Orchard, 2003) 266p. **Norway.** 🔲 YA 🔲 7.5

> Three young people from the quiet Medieval village of Spjothof find themselves caught up in a dangerous adventure as various groups of Vikings fight for supremacy of the northern lands.

Simner, Janni Lee. *Thief Eyes* (Random House, 2010) 272p. **Iceland.** 🔲 YA 🔲 5

> Sixteen-year-old Haley travels to Iceland to search for clues about her mother's mysterious disappearance and discovers some dangerous ancient magic.

Teller, Janne. *Nothing.* Trans. Martin Aiken (Atheneum, 2010) 240p. **Denmark.** 🔲 YA 🔲 8.5

> When a seventh-grade boy declares that life is meaningless, his classmates try to prove him wrong but end up in a vicious cycle of cruelty.

Eastern Europe Booktalks

In this section, Eastern Europe refers to the former Eastern Bloc countries of Poland, former Yugoslavia, Czechoslovakia, Hungary, Romania, Albania, and Lithuania. Although it's all one Europe now, this region has had a stormy political past. During World War II, Eastern Europe was the site of horrible Nazi death camps. There are stories of survivors and people who helped them, but the overwhelming tragedy of the Jewish Holocaust pervades. After the war, the people of Eastern Europe suffered poverty, restrictions, and human rights abuses under Communist rule. After the Communists left, the region was still unstable as the Bosnian War spurred a new genocide in several countries, including Kosovo, Albania, Croatia, Bosnia and Herzegovina, and Serbia. The one bright spot in this section is Marie Rutkoski's fantasy series set in Prague. If your students need a magical escapist fiction series after all this reality, I recommend The Kronos Chronicles.

Fiction

Boyne, John. *The Boy in the Striped Pajamas: A Fable* (David Fickling, 2006) 224p. **Poland.** **IL** 6–9 **RL** 8.3

When Bruno is nine years old, he and his family have to leave their beautiful house in Berlin and move to a desolate house in the middle of nowhere. Bruno doesn't understand why they had to leave, but he knows it has something to do with his father's important job, and "the Fury," a powerful man who sometimes comes to dinner at their house. Bruno is pretty miserable at first because he doesn't see any other houses or any way to meet other kids his age, but then he sees at the back of the house a barbed-wire fence with thousands of people, kids and adults, all wearing the same striped pajamas. Smart readers will guess that this is really Auschwitz, the Nazi concentration camp, but Bruno never figures it out. He becomes best friends with Boy, a Jew living in the camp, and they talk every day through the barbed wire that separates them. Their friendship has a tragic ending with a surprise twist. If you're paying attention, you will see it coming. This is not a true story; it's not really even believable that Bruno could be so naive, but it will definitely make you think.

Paterson, Katherine. *The Day of the Pelican* (Clarion, 2009) 145p. **Albania.** **IL** 5–8 **RL** 4.7

Twelve-year-old Meli is an Albanian living in Kosovo with her family in the late 1990s. She doesn't understand why the Serbians there hate the

Albanians, but she tries her best to keep away from them and not cause any trouble. But when her brother is kidnapped and the police won't help, she realizes that her family is not safe in Kosovo. After a few weeks, her brother miraculously comes home, but he is bitter and angry at the Serbs who beat him for no reason and left him to die. The family decides to leave the city, so they pack up their things and go to their farm in the country, but they are not safe there either, and eventually they have to run for their lives to get out of Kosovo before they are all killed. This story is based on true events that took place less than twenty years ago in Yugoslavia when Serbians carried out a policy of "ethnic cleansing" to eliminate the Muslim Albanian population in Kosovo.

Rutkoski, Marie. *The Cabinet of Wonders* (FSG, 2008) 258 pages. Czech Republic. IL 4–7 RL 3.9

This book will likely hook readers from the first chapter when the main character, Petra Kronos, is awoken by her mechanical pet spider. When she goes downstairs to feed a whole zoo of mechanical animals, I just knew this was going to be good. It turns out her father is a clock maker. He crafts lots of metallic objects and machines, and he has been away at Prince Rodolfo's castle in Prague building the finest clock the world has ever seen. But when he comes home with a bandage over his face, he tells Petra that the prince stole his eyes (Eww!) so he can pop them in his own eye sockets and see the world the way Kronos does. (Double Eww!) Just imagine the freakiness of seeing someone else wearing your father's eyes! Petra is so upset by this that she secretly goes to Prague to steal her father's eyes back. When she gets there, she meets a mischievous and hilarious gypsy boy who agrees to help her, and they go on a wild adventure to try to find where the prince keeps his extra eyes and figure out a plan for getting them out of the castle without anyone suspecting them. Along the way, they discover that the clock her father built has a secret that the prince is desperate to unlock, and if he does, it will give him a terrible, evil power. So then, of course, Petra has to deal with that, too. See also the sequel, *Book II of the Kronos Chronicles, The Celestial Globe* (FSG, 2010).

Spinelli, Jerry. *Milkweed* (Knopf, 2003) 224p. Poland. IL 4–7 RL 5.2

This book is about an orphan living in Poland in 1939. He has no home or family. He doesn't know how old he is or even his name because he never had anyone to tell him who he is. All anyone ever calls him is "Stopthief!" He lives by stealing food and sleeping in abandoned stores or anywhere he can find. He becomes friends with a little Jewish girl named Janina who gives him food. He doesn't know if he's Jewish or not, but when the Nazis round up all the Jews and force them to move to the ghetto, he goes too to be with Janina. Life is impossibly hard for the Jews in the ghetto, but our little orphan has never known any other life, so it's no different for him. He helps Janina's family by stealing food for them, and they give him something he never had—the comfort of a family.

Nonfiction

Halilbegovich, Nadja. *My Childhood Under Fire: A Sarajevo Diary* (Kids Can, 2006) 120p. **Bosnia and Herzegovina.** **IL** 5–9 **RL** 5.1

When she was twelve years old, Nadja's happy, normal childhood ended. The year was 1992, and Bosnians and Serbs were at war in Nadja's home city of Sarajevo. This is Nadja's actual diary from that time. In it she describes how she is afraid to sleep in her bed near the window because explosions outside could shatter the glass. She is afraid to go outside because anyone could be killed at any time by snipers or bombs anywhere in the city, even at school. Every day when her mother leaves for work, Nadja is afraid she won't come home. She never describes who is fighting or what they are fighting about because to Nadja, it doesn't matter. There is no cause for killing innocent people like kids who just want to go outside and play or simply cross the street without having to look both ways for snipers. If you have ever wondered what your life would be like if you had to live in a war zone, this book gives you a very real picture.

Krinitz, Esther Nisenthal, and Bernice Steinhadt. *Memories of Survival* (Hyperion, 2005) 64p. **Poland.** **IL** 4–8 **RL** 5

In 1942, Nazi soldiers ordered that everyone in Esther's neighborhood in Poland had to leave their home and go to the train station where they would be sent away forever. If they refused to go, the Nazis shot them. Esther and her sister got separated from their family. Alone and with no home to go to, they snuck away and hid in the forest. Eventually they found a kind couple who hid them in their barn, and the girls stayed with them, pretending they weren't Jewish. This is Esther's true story of how she and her sister were able to hide and survive the Holocaust. But they never saw anyone else from their family again.

Y Orlev, Uri. *Run, Boy, Run.* Trans. Hillel Halkin (Houghton Mifflin, 2003) 186p. **Poland.** **IL** 5–9 **RL** 5.8. Batchelder Honor

This is the true story of a boy trying to survive the Jewish Holocaust. Eight-year-old Srulik lives in the Warsaw ghetto with his family. When they get separated, Srulik doesn't know what to do, so he joins a gang of street orphans who steal food to survive. One day they see the soldiers lining up all the Jews and forcing them onto trains for "resettlement." The kids don't know exactly what that means, but they know it's not good, so they run away and escape the ghetto. Srulik gets separated again, and now he is alone in the Polish countryside with no food, no money, and no family in a place where being Jewish is a crime. His only hope is to pretend to be Christian and try to work for a Polish farmer. But if he gets found out, he will be killed for sure. If you like suspenseful action-filled survival stories, this one will have you on the edge of your seat!

Roy, Jennifer. *Yellow Star* (Marshall Cavendish, 2006) 227p. **Poland.** **IL** 5–9 **RL** 6.1

In 1939, the Germans invaded the town of Lodz, Poland, and the entire Jewish population was forced to leave their homes and move into a small, enclosed part of the city called a ghetto. At the end of the war, there were only eight hundred survivors from that ghetto, and of those, only twelve were children. This is the true story told by Syvia, one of the child survivors. The Germans were removing all of the children from the ghetto to go to another camp, a death camp. Syvia's parents didn't know where all the children were going, but they were not about to hand their daughter over to the Nazis, so they found ingenious and sometimes lucky ways to hide her. One night when the Nazis came looking for children, Syvia's father took her out the back door to a cemetery. He dug a grave and they stayed inside it until the Nazis stopped looking for them. But after that, Syvia had to hide in the house because if the soldiers ever caught a glimpse of her, they would send her away. This is an amazing true story about how Syvia hid right under the soldiers' noses for five years until the war ended.

Rubin, Susan Goldman, and Ela Weissberger. *The Cat with the Yellow Star: Coming of Age in Terezin* (Holiday House, 2006) 40p. **Poland.** **IL** 3–6 **RL** 4.8

In 1942, eleven-year-old Ela and all the other Jews in Prague, Czechoslovakia, were forced to leave their homes and get on Nazi trains to concentration camps. Ela and her family were sent to Terezin Camp. The conditions in the camp were horrible; the people were cold and hungry—and terrified of the Nazi soldiers. But they also made the best of their time there by helping to cheer each other up, drawing, singing, and even performing an opera. Ela played the part of the cat in the opera, the cat with the yellow star because Jews had to wear a yellow star. After four years in the camp, the war ended, and the prisoners were set free. Many did not survive, but Ela did, and she went on to serve in the army in Israel, and then get married and move to America.

Eastern Europe Book List

This list contains additional important stories about Jewish Holocaust survival and life after World War II. Although there are several books suitable for teaching younger kids about this topic, the books included in the Grades 7 and up list are more intense. I hope the twenty-first century has happier stories to tell about this region.

Fiction

Cheng, Andrea. *The Bear Makers* (Front Street, 2008) 176p. **Hungary.** IL 5–8 RL 3

Based on the true story of the author's grandmother, this book describes the life of a young girl and her family in post–World War II Budapest. They survived the war, but now the Hungarian Worker's Party policies are making life very difficult for them.

Gleitzman, Morris. *Once* (Henry Holt, 2010) 176p. **Poland.** IL 6–9

Felix, a ten-year-old Jewish boy, has been hidden from the Nazis in a Catholic orphanage or the last four years, but he risks his safety to try to find his parents.

Hesse, Karen. *The Cats in Krasinski Square.* Illus. Wendy Watson (Scholastic, 2004) 32p. **Poland.** IL 3–5 RL 4.7

This picture book tells the story of two Jewish sisters who escape from the ghetto and secretly smuggle food to the starving people who still live behind the dark wall.

Nonfiction

Andronik, Catherine M. *Copernicus: Founder of Modern Astronomy* (Enslow, 2002) 112p. **Poland.** IL 4–8 RL 7

Describes the life of the famous Polish astronomer Nicolaus Kopernik, who later Latinized his name to Copernicus.

Bogacki, Tomek. *The Champion of Children: The Story of Janusz Korczak* (FSG, 2009) 32p. **Poland.** **IL** 4–7 **RL** 6.3

This picture book tells the true story of Janusz Korczak who maintained his Jewish children's orphanage even in the ghetto in Poland until they were all sent to a Nazi concentration camp.

Levine, Karen. *Hana's Suitcase* (Albert Whiman, 2003) 111p. **Czech Republic.** **IL** 4–7 **RL** 5.2

The suitcase of Czech girl Hana, who died in the Jewish Holocaust, ends up at the Tokyo Holocaust Education Resource Center and inspires the curator to learn about Hana's life.

Molnar, Haya Leah. *Under a Red Sky: Memoir of a Childhood in Communist Russia* (FSG, 2010) 320p. **Romania.** **IL** 5–8 **RL** 5.6

The author recounts her memories of growing up in Romania during the late 1950s.

♥ Sís, Peter. *The Wall: Growing Up Behind the Iron Curtain* (FSG, 2007) 48p. **Czech Republic.** **IL** 5–8 **RL** 4.3. Caldecott Honor, Sibert Medal

This memoir describes what it was like to grow up, with very little freedom of expression, in Soviet-controlled Czechoslovakia during the 1960s.

Taylor, Peter Lane. *The Secret of Priest's Grotto: A Holocaust Survival Story* (Kar Ben, 2007) 64p. **Poland.** **IL** 5–9 **RL** 7

During World War II, a group of Jewish refugees survived the Holocaust by living in underground caves. This is the amazing true story.

Vander Zee, Ruth. *Eli Remembers.* Illus. Bill Farnsworth (Eerdmans, 2007) 32p. **Lithuania.** **IL** 3–5 **RL** 3.5

In this picture book, Eli visits the site of his ancestors' murder in Lithuania during the Jewish Holocaust and for the first time understands his family's sadness at Rosh Hashanah.

Grades 7 and Up—Fiction

Friedman, D. Dina. *Escaping into the Night* (Simon & Schuster, 2006) 199p. **Poland.** **IL** YA **RL** 4

Halina is thirteen years old when she runs away from the Polish ghetto and is taken in by a secret resistance group living in the forest. This is a fictionalized story of actual forest camps that sheltered Jews during World War II.

Marillier, Juliet. *Wildwood Dancing* (Knopf, 2007) 407p. **Romania.** IL YA RL 4.3

Five sisters living with their father in a Transylvanian castle called Piscul Draculi discover a secret magical world, the Wildwood, which they can only access during the full moon. See also the sequel *Cybele's Secret* (Knopf, 2008).

Grades 7 and Up—Nonfiction

Y **Warren, Andre.** *Surviving Hitler: A Boy in the Nazi Death Camps* (HarperCollins, 2001) 146p. **Poland.** IL YA RL 6.2. Sibert Honor

The true story of Jack Mandelbaum, a fourteen-year-old Polish boy who was separated from his parents when Nazis invaded Poland and survived four years in Nazi concentration camps.

Chapter 4

South and Central America

South America Booktalks

How people first got to South America is a mystery, but it is clear from archaeological evidence that they were there for a long time, since at least 6500 B.C.E. Over the years, they started farming and cultivating animals such as llamas and built a powerful empire in the Andes Mountains. Kids will be fascinated by stories of the battles between the Inca and Pizarro's troops of conquistadors from Spain. Also fascinating are the stories of elusive Amazon creatures such as tarantulas and pink dolphins that make you wonder what else is out there that we don't even know about.

Fiction

Doder, Joshua. *Grk and the Pelotti Gang* (Delacorte, 2006) 193p. Brazil. ▨
3–6 **RL** 3.3

The Pelotti gang includes three Brazilian brothers who have robbed millions from banks all across Brazil. No one has been able to catch them until Max and Natascha Raffifi's father succeeds. But now Mr. Raffifi is dead, and Max, Natascha, and their dog Grk live with Tim Malt and his parents. When the Pelotti gang escapes from prison, Max, Natascha, and Tim decide to go to Brazil and stop them. Of course, they bring their brave and intelligent dog Grk along to help. Well, who knows how three kids and a dog thought they would just jump on a plane to Rio and single-handedly catch an armed and dangerous gang of criminals, but anyway, things don't go as planned and Tim and Grk end up being kidnapped and held for ransom by some street kids. Coincidentally, the kids lead them straight to the Pelotti gang! So now that Tim and Grk have them, the problem is not so much how to bring the gang to justice but how to get home alive! See also the other books in the Grk series.

Ibbotson, Eva. *Journey to the River Sea.* Illus. Kevin Hawkes (Dutton, 2001) 298p. **Brazil.** ⬛ 3–7 ⬛ 5.9

Maia is a wealthy orphan at boarding school, and when she finds out she has family in Brazil, Mr. and Mrs. Carter and their twin daughters, who want to take her in, she gets really excited to go to the Amazon. Of course she can't go all that way by herself, so her solicitor hires a governess to travel with her and be her teacher in Brazil. Miss Minton is very strict, but Maia wins her over, and they become good friends. Sadly, she does not become friends with the Carters. The twins are spoiled and selfish, and the greedy parents only want Maia for the money they get from her solicitor. Maia tries to make the best of it, but she is pretty miserable, and there is nothing Miss Minton can do because she is afraid of losing her job. Maia wants to go exploring and learn about the country and people there, but she is not allowed to do anything . . . until she wins the trust of the native people who let her in on a secret. There is a boy her age living alone in the jungle, and they are hiding him from the British investigators who want to force him back to England. Maia and her new friend come up with a plot that will let everyone live happily ever.

Skarmeta, Antonio. *The Composition.* Illus. Alfonso Ruano (Groundwood, 2000) 32p. ⬛ 3–6 ⬛ 3.5

A dictatorship is a government in which a country's people are not allowed to say anything against the government or read newspapers, listen to the radio or watch television programs that say anything bad about the government. If the people disobey the government, they could be arrested, tortured, put in prison, or even killed for no reason. In a country ruled by a dictator, there may be spies everywhere to tell on you if you do anything that the government doesn't like. This book is about a boy named Pedro who lives in a dictatorship in South America, and the sneaky way the government tries to get him to tell on his parents. Every night his parents listen to a foreign radio news station. They are not hurting anyone, but they always keep the volume very low so no one can hear because if any spies found out, they could be arrested. One day a soldier comes to school and tells the kids to write a two-or three-page composition, or an essay, for a contest. The winner will get a gold medal. The topic is to write about what your parents do at home after work. That's all. Just write in detail all the TV shows they watch, what they read, what friends come over, and what they talk about. Pedro is only nine years old. Will he tell the truth about what his parents do at night, or will he realize that it's a trap, and the government is going to read these compositions to see whose parents are disobeying their unfair laws?

Nonfiction

Kops, Deborah. *Machu Picchu* (Twenty-First Century, 2009) 80p. **Peru.** **IL** 4–8 **RL** 5.8

In the 1400s, the Inca built a beautiful city called Machu Picchu high in the Andes Mountains of Peru. They deserted the city when the Spanish conquerors came, and over time the city was completely forgotten and overgrown. Then in the 1900s, Hiram Bingham, an explorer who was interested in South American history, went to Peru to look for old Inca ruins. He had no idea what he would find, but some locals tipped him off and he ended up discovering Machu Picchu. This book describes their trek through the jungle across rivers on rickety log bridges, and the long, hard climb up the mountains at altitudes so high, they were in the clouds. It also describes and shows pictures of this amazing ancient city.

Kras, Sara Louise. *The Galapagos Islands* (Marshall Cavendish, 2009) 96p. **Ecuador.** **IL** 4–8 **RL** 6

The Galapagos are a group of islands in the Pacific Ocean 600 miles off the coast of Ecuador on the continent of South America. They were formed entirely by volcanoes erupting under the ocean. As the lava cooled, it formed land, and the islands popped up out of the ocean. You would think that if an island just appeared out of the ocean, no land animals would live there. After all, how would they get there? So the only animals native to the islands either swam there or flew there, but if you go, you will be able to see some species that live nowhere else in the world. This book describes the giant turtles, the penguins, the iguanas, and the blue-footed birds that make the islands their home. The book also talks about how, if we destroy their homes, these animals will have literally nowhere else to go. They will become extinct, so protecting the Galapagos Islands is extremely important.

Lourie, Peter. *Lost Treasure of the Inca* (Boyds Mill, 1999) 48p. **Ecuador.** 🔲 5–7 **RL** 6.2

This book is about the largest treasure in the world: 750 tons of Inca gold is buried somewhere in the Andes Mountains. What happened was, in 1532, Francisco Pizarro and the Spanish conquistadors came to South America to conquer the Inca lands and steal their gold. They captured Atahualpa, the Inca king, and promised to release him if he could fill a huge room with gold. So all of Atahualpa's generals started bringing gold from all over the Incan Empire, but Pizarro killed Atahualpa anyway, and when the generals found out, they hid the gold so Pizarro would never find it. For four hundred years, people have been searching the Andes to try and find the gold, but no one has ever found it and lived. This book is about one man who had a treasure map, and he went to Ecuador to try to find the gold. He didn't find it, but the book includes the map, so if you want to go to Ecuador yourself and try to find the treasure, you can.

▄ Video Booktalk: http://www.bookwink.com/archive_2008_07_13.html

Montgomery, Sy. *Encantado: Pink Dolphin of the Amazon.* Photog. Dianne Taylor-Snow (Houghton Mifflin, 2002) 73p. 🔲 4–7 **RL** 5

The picture on this cover is not fake. That's a real dolphin, and it's really bubblegum pink! You may be wondering, "Is that a freak of nature? A mutant caused by swimming in nuclear waste?" No, they are actually very ancient relatives of the whale, and they live in the fresh water of the Amazon. Scientists know very little about them, but locals call them *encantados,* meaning the enchanted ones, and there are lots of folk stories about them. In this book, you will travel to the Amazon where there are huge man-eating snakes, poisonous tarantulas, vicious piranhas, electric eels, spider webs as big as badminton nets, and who knows what else! There you will follow the author on her quest to discover more about these mysterious pink dolphins.

♟ **Montgomery, Sy.** *The Tarantula Scientist.* Photog. Nic Bishop (Houghton Mifflin, 2004) 80p. **French Guiana.** 🔲 4–8 **RL** 5.6. Sibert Honor

If you have arachnophobia—fear of spiders—this book will probably make you run screaming. There are lots of up close and personal photos of tarantulas that look like they could crawl off the page and attack you! But tarantulas don't actually attack humans. They do attack other things though. If you were a tiny insect in the jungle, the tarantula would seem like a ferocious jaguar. They are really cool animals, and this book takes you to the tropical rainforest of South America with an American scientist who spends all his time studying them. Scientists don't actually know very much about tarantulas, but this book does give you some good details about how they take down their prey, what their houses are like, and even how they poop. So if you're interested in that, you will love this book!

South America Book List

Although parts of South America are modern and wealthy, there are still remote areas where natives live much as they have for generations. Several books in this list explore contemporary life for people who still maintain their culture.

Fiction

Durango, Julia. *The Walls of Cartagena.* Illus. Tom Pohrt (Simon & Schuster, 2008) 160p. **Colombia.** **IL** 4–7 **RL** 5.2

The adventures of a thirteen-year-old slave named Calepino bring to light the horrors of the slave trade and the Spanish Inquisition in seventeenth-century Colombia.

Foreman, Michael. *Mia's Story: A Sketchbook of Hopes and Dreams* (Candlewick, 2006) 32p. **Chile.** **IL** 1–4 **RL** 3

In this picture book, while looking for her beloved puppy, Mia discovers a way to make her village more lovely and her family's life easier.

Hussey, Charmian. *The Valley of Secrets* (Simon & Schuster, 2005) 370p. **IL** 6–9 **RL** 6.5

When his great uncle dies and leaves him his estate, Stephen uncovers family secrets and discovers a whole new world by reading his great uncle's Amazon travel journal.

Nelson, N.A. *Bringing the Boy Home* (HarperCollins, 2008) 224p. **IL** 4–7 **RL** 3.9

As two Takunami boys approach their thirteenth birthdays, Luka prepares for the tribe's manhood test while Tirio, adopted and raised in

Miami, Florida, feels pressure to prove himself during his upcoming visit to the Amazon rain forest where he was born.

Rand, Gloria. *A Pen Pal for Max.* Illus. Ted Rand (Henry Holt, 2005) 32p. **Chile.** ⬛ K–4 ⬛ 4

In this picture book, the son of a Chilean farmer writes a note asking for a pen pal and places it in a box of grapes bound for the United States.

Ryan, Pam Muñoz. *The Dreamer.* Illus. Peter Sís (Scholastic, 2010) 384p. **Chile.** ⬛ 6–9 ⬛ 3.7

This book imagines the childhood of Chilean poet, Pablo Neruda.

Nonfiction

Braman, Arlette M. *Secrets of Ancient Cultures: The Inca, Activities and Crafts from a Mysterious Land.* Illus. Michele Nidenhoff (Wiley, 2004) 113p. **Peru, Ecuador.** ⬛ 3–6

History combines with craft projects, recipes, games, and activities to help you explore the Incan culture.

🏆 **Brown, Monica.** *My Name Is Gabito: The Life of Gabriel García Márquez.* Illus. Raul Colon (Rising Moon, 2007) 32p. **Colombia.** ⬛ 3–6 ⬛ 5.9. Pura Belpré Honor

This picture book biography tells of the famous author's childhood in Colombia.

Calvert, Patricia. *The Ancient Inca* (Franklin Watts, 2004) 128p. **Peru, Ecuador.** ⬛ 5–8 ⬛ 7.6

This book gives you a sense of what life was like for the ancient Inca living in Peru and Ecuador.

Dingus, Lowell, Luis M. Chiappe, and Rodolfo Coria. *Dinosaur Eggs Discovered!: Unscrambling the Clues* (Twenty-First Century, 2007) 112p. **Argentina.** ⬛ 5–8

The three authors describe their paleontology expedition to Argentina to look for bird fossils, but they make an unexpected discovery instead. They find an area full of fossilized dinosaur eggs that lead to some new information about the prehistoric creatures.

Mann, Charles C. *Before Columbus: The Americas of 1491* (Atheneum, 2009) 116p. **IL** 6–9 **RL** 9.2

This book uses research from the past two decades to challenge some of the long-held beliefs about early civilizations of South and Central America. It gives a fascinating picture of life in the Americas before and during the arrival of Europeans.

Quinlan, Susan E. *The Case of the Monkeys That Fell from the Trees: And Other Mysteries in Tropical Nature* (Boyds Mill, 2010) 171p. **IL** 4–7 **RL** 7.5

This book explains some of the scientific mysteries of the tropical forests of South and Central America. For example, why do monkeys sometimes just fall out of their trees? And how do poison dart frogs make their poison?

Grades 7 and Up—Fiction

Abelove, Joan. *Go and Come Back* (Penguin, 1998) 177p. **Peru. IL** YA **RL** 5.2

In a remote village in the Peruvian jungle, Alicia, an Isabo girl, describes the odd behavior of the two white ladies who have come from New York as anthropologists to live with the tribe and study them.

Peet, Mal. *Keeper* (Candlewick, 2003) 225p. **IL** YA **RL** 7.1

When Paul Faustino, the best sportswriter in South America, interviews El Gato, the phenomenal goalkeeper who single-handedly brought his team the World Cup, he hears a strange story about a mysterious mentor in the jungle, "the Keeper," who teaches El Gato everything he knows about soccer.

Resau, Laura. *The Indigo Notebook* (Delacorte, 2009) 324p. **Ecuador. IL** YA **RL** 4.7

Fifteen-year-old Zeeta has never met her father and has never lived in one country for more than a year. After moving to Ecuador, she hopes her mother will finally settle down and decide to live a normal life.

Whelan, Gloria. *The Disappeared* (Dial, 2008) 144p. **Argentina. IL** YA **RL** 4.5

When Silvia's brother is kidnapped by the Argentinian government, she enters a dangerous world in her attempt to rescue him.

Central America Booktalks

Several of the books in this section attest to the human rights violations that took place during the long and brutal war in Guatemala that ended in 1996. Many of the victims were native Mayans, an indigenous group that has lived in Mexico and Central America for thousands of years. For more books about the ancient Mayan civilization, please see the chapter on North America.

Fiction

Cameron, Ann. *Colibri* (FSG, 2003) 227p. **Guatemala.** ■ 5–8 **RL** 6.1

When she was four years old, Colibri was kidnapped by a beggar in Guatemala City. He changed her name to Rosa and forced her to call him Uncle, and he used her to get more pity from the people who felt sorry enough for them to give them money. Uncle was a liar and a cheat, but he never abused Rosa because a fortuneteller told him that their fortunes were intertwined, that Rosa would bring him a huge treasure if he treated her well. So he has been waiting and waiting for this fortune to come true, for Rosa to make him rich, but now he is starting to give up on her. She has no hope of ever finding her parents again. If Uncle abandons her, she will be out on the streets alone to fend for herself. How will she survive, and how will she ever get a better life?

Mikaelson, Ben. *Red Midnight* (HarperCollins, 2002) 212p. **Guatemala.** ■ 5–8 **RL** 5.4

Santiago is twelve years old when the soldiers come to his village in Guatemala and burn it to the ground, killing everyone. He and his four-year-old sister are the only survivors, and if the soldiers find them, they will kill them, too. The only way to be safe is to leave Guatemala and sail to America. So now they are running for their lives, trying to get to the coast where their uncle has a boat they can take. But once they get on the water, the real danger begins. Santiago has sailed only once. How will he make a three-week trip through shark-infested water, where there are pirates and strong currents that could sweep him out into the Atlantic Ocean to his death? How will he get enough food and water for him and his little sister? If you like books about adventure and survival, you'll love this one.

Pellegrino, Marge. *Journey of Dreams* (Frances Lincoln, 2009) 250p. **Guatemala.** `IL` 5–8 `RL` 4.5

    The year is 1984 and guerilla soldiers are fighting against the government in Guatemala. Tomasa lives with her family in a village in the mountains. She doesn't know what the fighting is about. All she knows is she doesn't want it to come to her village . . . but it does anyway. First government soldiers come and round up all the boys who are old enough to fight. Then her mother leaves with her oldest brother so he won't have to join the army. It's not safe to say anything against the government, so Tomasa and her father keep quiet and secretly plan to leave. But the soldiers are watching them closely for any signs of rebellion, and one night they attack the village and destroy it. Will Tomasa be able to escape? Will she ever see her mother and older brother again? Read this book to find out about her harrowing flight to freedom.

Central America Book List

    Part of Central America is considered to be a biodiversity hotspot, an area of super abundant plant and animal life that is extremely threatened by humans. The books in this list tell a little more about this amazing region.

Nonfiction

Mann, Charles C. *Before Columbus: The Americas of 1491* (Atheneum, 2009) 116p. `IL` 6–9 `RL` 9.2

    This book uses research from the past two decades to challenge some of the long-held beliefs about early civilizations of South and Central America. It gives a fascinating picture of life in the Americas before and during the arrival of Europeans.

Quinlan, Susan E. *The Case of the Monkeys That Fell from the Trees: And Other Mysteries in Tropical Nature* (Boyds Mill, 2010) 171p. `IL` 4–7 `RL` 7.5

    This book explains some of the scientific mysteries of the tropical forests of South and Central America. For example, why do monkeys sometimes just fall out of their trees? And how do poison dart frogs make their poison?

Grades 7 and Up—Fiction

Resau, Laura. *Red Glass* (Delacorte, 2007) 304p. **Guatemala.** ⬛ YA 🟥 4.8

Sixteen-year-old Sophie's life changes when her family takes in a six-year-old Guatemalan orphan. Before they can adopt him, they travel to Guatemala to see if he has any relatives who would claim him. Along the way, Sophie falls in love and sees a harsher reality than she has ever experienced in America.

Chapter 5

North America

Canada Booktalks

Canada is the world's second largest country, but not nearly the most populous. There is still lots of wide-open space filled with animals such as caribou, moose, elk, bears and . . . snakes. Populated for millennia by native people, like the United States, it was colonized by Europeans in the 1500s. Some of the themes of Canadian history feel similar to those of U.S. history, like westward expansion and industrialization, and the contemporary fiction feels very similar to contemporary fiction set in the United States. But one major difference that is important to point out to students is that while the United States was actively allowing slavery, Canada abolished slavery and became a safe haven for escaped slaves.

Fiction

♈ **Curtis, Christopher Paul.** *Elijah of Buxton* (Scholastic, 2007) 341p. ▣ 4–7
▣ 7.8. Newbery Honor, Coretta Scott King Medal, Jane Addams Honor
    If you like your books to be a combination of funny and serious, then you will love *Elijah of Buxton*. The year is 1859, and eleven-year-old Elijah Freeman lives in Buxton, Canada, which is a haven for freed and escaped

slaves. Elijah is famous in his town because he is the first child in the town who was born free (not a slave) and also because when he was a baby, he threw up all over the famous speaker Frederick Douglass. Elijah has some hilarious adventures with his friends, but things get serious when he discovers that the preacher who took their neighbor, Mr. Leroy's, life savings promising to help buy his family's freedom actually kept the money for himself. Elijah takes matters into his own hands to try to get Mr. Leroy's money back, but he discovers that the world outside Buxton is a very scary and dangerous place.

Jocelyn, Marthe. *Mable Riley: A Reliable Record of Humdrum, Peril, and Romance* (Candlewick, 2004) 279p. **IL** 4-7 **RL** 5.6

The year is 1901, and fourteen-year-old Mable Riley is leaving home with her older sister Viola to a new town in Ontario where Viola will be the schoolteacher. Mable will be a scholar in her school and will also help with the younger kids, but what she is most looking forward to is having adventures to write about. She wants to be a writer, so Mable writes down everything she sees and experiences, all the local gossip, the school quarrels and flirtations, and the goings-on at the women's Reading Club, which isn't a reading club at all but a secret society of suffragists. She also writes a scandalous romance novel in her free time. This book might remind some readers of *Anne of Green Gables,* also set in Canada. Mable and Anne are very different, but Mable is one of those characters you just want to cheer for, and even the mean characters in this book aren't so bad—they're only human. If you like historical fiction with happy endings, this book is for you!

Little, Jean. *Dancing through the Snow* (Kane Miller, 2009) 242p. **IL** 5–8 **RL** 4.6

Min was abandoned as a little girl, just dumped by her parents. Since then, she has lived in four different foster homes, and each one of them dumped her too, for one reason or another. Min has learned not to let her feelings show, not to cry or let anyone know that she is upset. She never even speaks unless she absolutely has to. This way, she can protect herself. If she keeps everything inside, then she won't lose any part of herself the next time she gets dumped. But her newest foster mother, Jess Hart, is different. Jess was abandoned as a child herself and grew up in foster homes too, so she understands how Min feels. This is a game-changer for Min. For the first time in her life, she feels safe and understood, but can she trust Jess, or will she dump her just like all the other adults in Min's life so far?

🏆 **Porter, Pamela.** *The Crazy Man* (Groundwood, 2005) 214p. ⬛ 5–8 🔲 4. Jane Addams Honor

Prejudice is when you judge people without really knowing them. Sometimes it can be because of their skin or because of their religion, how they dress, where they are from, or where they live. Any time you make a negative judgment about someone before you get to know them, you are being prejudiced. Well, when Emaline's father leaves and doesn't come back, her mother decides to hire someone to help on their farm. She hires Angus, a patient at the local mental hospital, and then they all learn how ugly prejudice can be. At first, Emaline is scared of Angus. Why was he in the mental hospital? Is he a deranged lunatic? A dangerous criminal? But as she gets to know him, she realizes that he is a gentle and good person who would never hurt anyone. Unfortunately, other people in the community don't believe that and don't think twice about tormenting him. They don't like him living in their community and will stop at nothing to get rid of him.

Wynne-Jones, Tim. *Rex Zero and the End of the World* (FSG, 2007) 186p. ⬛ 4–7 🔲 3.7

Rex is ten years old when his family moves to Ottawa, Canada. He doesn't know anyone, so he rides his bike around looking for stuff to do. Rex is kind of a spy-in-training and he notices that there are no kids around. Where are all the kids? One night while walking his dog in the park, his dog starts going crazy and Rex sees some strange flashes in the distance. Suddenly, a wild beast jumps out of the bushes and runs away. It turns out the flashes were from a girl named Kathy's camera, and she was trying to get pictures of whatever was in the bushes because none of the adults believe it's there. Now Rex can put his spy skills to real use! Can they figure out what that creature is and convince the adults before it attacks someone? Read this book to find out. See also the sequels *Rex Zero, the King of Nothing* (FSG, 2008) and *Rex Zero, the Great Pretender* (FSG, 2010).

Nonfiction

Greenwood, Barbara. *Factory Girl* (Kids Can, 2007) 136p. ⬛ 4–8 🔲 5.2

Imagine instead of being free and comfortable in your classroom all day, you have to quit school and work in a factory. Instead of a kind and caring teacher (☺), you have to deal with a mean factory boss yelling and blowing cigar smoke in your face. You might think that sounds better than homework, but working ten hours a day—Saturdays too —gets old really fast. This is the story of a girl named Emily who has to do just that, and you can see how hard her life is. Without the money she makes at the factory, her family will not be able to pay rent or buy food. If she messes up even a tiny bit, then precious money is deducted from her measly $4 pay. Some girls even have so much deducted that they get paid nothing after working all week long! It's also dangerous, and when a fire breaks out, Emily is one of the lucky ones who makes it out alive. Emily's story is fictional, but this book includes pictures of real factory kids and facts about real kids' lives during this time. In cities all across Canada and the United States during the 1900s, young girls worked in these horrible conditions because it was the only way to stay alive. After you read this book, you will be grateful for your easy life at school!

Heuer, Karsten. *Being Caribou: Five Months on Foot with a Caribou Herd* (Walker, 2007) 48p. **IL** 4–8 **RL** 6

Every year, huge herds of caribou migrate thousands of miles across Canada to the Arctic National Wildlife Refuge in Alaska to give birth to their calves. Then after a few days when the baby caribou can walk, they go all the way back. Why do they do this? Why is that one spot in Alaska so important that the caribou travel all that way? Well, the author of this book wanted to find out, so he and his wife planned a five-month journey walking and skiing through the wilderness to follow the caribou. This book describes their trudge through deep snow and blizzards, their scary encounters with wolves and grizzly bears, watching a baby calf being born and taking its first steps, and then the swarms of bugs that forced them all to leave, making the long journey home again to Canada. If you are interested in wildlife or remote wilderness camping, you will love this book, adapted from an adult book with the same title.

Montgomery, Sy. *The Snake Scientist.* Photog. Nic Bishop (Houghton Mifflin, 1999) 48p. **IL** 3–8 **RL** 6.7

Every spring at the Narcisse Wildlife Management Area in Manitoba, Canada, thousands of garter snakes wake up from their eight-month hibernation under ground, and pour out above ground, "a river of writhing reptiles!" There are so many snakes, you can't even see the ground—it just looks like the ground is moving. This is the true story of Bob Mason, a snake scientist who travels to Manitoba every year to study the snakes. This book answers all your snake questions such as: Why are all those snakes in one place? Why does a snake flick its tongue in and out? What does it feel like to hold a snake? The book also includes some absolutely amazing photos like the one where the snake is eating a tadpole. If you like snakes, you have to read this book. And even if you are not a snake lover, this book is still really cool.

Canada Book List

Like the United States, Canada is a nation of immigrants, so these books chronicle some of that history and reflect the diversity in Canada today.

Fiction

Baker, Deirdre. *Becca at Sea* (Groundwood, 2007) 165p. **IL** 4–6 **RL** 4

While her parents are away, Becca spends time with her grandmother who lives on a small island off Vancouver.

Ellis, Sarah. *Odd Man Out* (Groundwood, 2006) 162p. **IL** 5–7 **RL** 3.3

Kip spends the summer with his grandmother in British Columbia and finds a treasure, an old binder that once belonged to his dead father.

Walters, Eric. *War of the Eagles* (Orca, 1998) 224p. **IL** 5–8 **RL** 3.9

Jed's world is severely shaken after the attack on Pearl Harbor when his best friend is sent to detention camp in central Canada along with the rest of the Japanese-Canadian community. See also the sequel, *Caged Eagles* (Orca, 2000).

Nonfiction

Guiberson, Brenda Z. *Life in the Boreal Forest.* Illus. Gennady Spirin (Henry Holt, 2009) 32p. **IL** 3–5 **RL** 5.6

This picture book illustrates the boreal forest at Earth's far north and the creatures that live there throughout the year.

Hughes, Susan. *Coming to Canada: Building a Life in a New Land* (Maple Tree, 2005) 111p. **IL** 5–8 **RL** 7

This book chronicles the history of immigration to Canada, from the founding of Quebec in 1608.

Perkins, Lynne Rae. *Pictures from Our Vacation* (Greenwillow, 2007) 32p. **IL** 2–5 **RL** 3.5

> A young girl documents her trip to visit relatives in Canada.

Grade 7 and Up—Fiction

Frost, Helen. *The Braid* (FSG, 2006) 95p. **IL** YA **RL** 4

> Two sisters living in Scotland in the 1850s get separated when their family is forcibly evicted and deported. The older sister stays behind in Scotland and falls in love, while the younger sister starts a new life as an immigrant in Cape Breton, Canada.

Larson, Hope. *Mercury* (Atheneum, 2010) 240p. **IL** YA **RL** 2

> This graphic novel weaves together the stories of two girls living in Nova Scotia, one in modern times and one in 1859.

Mexico Booktalks

Mexico is the most populous Spanish-speaking country in the world. This plus its rich history dating back to prehistoric Mayan times make it fun to study for a Spanish language class. This is one part of the book where I stray from the current political borders. In this section are books set in Mexican California and Texas before they became part of the United States. Even though this part of the world is not Mexico today, it is still essential to a study of Mexican history.

Fiction

🏆 **Ryan, Pam Muñoz.** *Becoming Naomi León* (Scholastic, 2004) 246p. **IL** 4-7 **RL** 5. Pura Belpré Honor

> Naomi Soledad León Outlaw's life with Gram and her little brother, Owen, is happy and peaceful until their mother reappears after seven years of absence. Naomi's mother is flighty and unreliable, and her boyfriend Clive is greedy and conniving. Naomi doesn't trust them and she definitely doesn't want to leave Gram to go live with them. But when her mother threatens to fight for custody in court, Gram takes drastic measures. Naomi's only memory of her father is the night of the hurricane when they got separated and she never saw him again. But Gram knows he is still alive somewhere in Mexico, and he is their last hope of protecting the kids from their mother. So Gram takes Owen and Naomi on a road trip to Mexico to

try and find him. This book may bring tears to some readers' eyes, and it will totally make you want to visit Mexico!

Wood, Frances M. *Daughter of Madrugada* (Delacorte, 2002) 162p. ▮ 4–7 ▮ 4

In 1846, California was not part of the United States; it was a part of Mexico. Thirteen-year-old Cesa de Haro lives there with her family. They own Madrugada Ranch—acres and acres of land with an entire village of *vaqueros* (Spanish for cowboys) to take care of their thousands of cattle. With all of the land and cattle they own and servants they employ, the de Haros are definitely upper-class Mexicans. But when Mexico loses the Mexican-American War, Americans think they have the right to take over the de Haro's land. Once gold is discovered in the California hills, the problem gets even worse as more and more poor white Americans come in droves and just start building their own houses, fences, and everything else right in the middle of Madrugada Ranch. What can the de Haros do to stop them? Do they have any rights to their own land, or is their only choice just to watch as other people steal it out from under them? This is not a true story, but it is based on the history of California.

Nonfiction

Freedman, Russell. *In the Days of the Vaqueros: America's First True Cowboys* (Clarion, 2001) 70p. ▮ 4–8 ▮ 7.9

When you think of cowboys, you think of American heroes riding bravely across the Wild West. But this book tells you all about the first cowboys, the Mexican *vaqueros* (pronounced va-KEH-rohs) who taught the American cowboys everything they knew. Without the *vaqueros,* Americans wouldn't know how to tame wild horses, lasso cattle, or ride bucking broncos. It was such a part of many Mexican boys' lives that they rode horses as soon as they could walk, and most could lasso a chicken by the time they were six or seven years old. As they grew up, they learned how to round up the cattle and tame wild *mesteños* (pronounced mes-stehn-yos), or as Americans call them, mustangs. This book shows how every part of our modern rodeo comes from the dangerous work the Mexican *vaqueros* did every day.

Orr, Tamra. *The Maya* (Franklin Watts, 2005) 64p. ▮ 4-7

The Maya were one of the great ancient civilizations in the Americas. Their culture was advanced, but also savage. One of the savage things they did was to conduct human sacrifices. They believed in offering blood as a gift to their gods, so they would practice "bloodletting," sometimes cutting themselves, and sometimes sacrificing a human slave. They also played a ball game similar to soccer, except they would play against their enemies, and the losing team was killed after the game—and not in the metaphorical sense like "Yeah, we killed the other team!" No, the players actually died if they lost. Think about that at your next soccer game! But the Maya also made some incredible advances in technology. They built huge pyramids, and they had a very detailed and sophisticated calendar. They also had the amazingly brilliant idea of eating chocolate. They drank it in liquid form and called it the drink of the gods—hot chocolate! They knew a good thing when they found it! Mayan descendents are still alive today in Mexico, Guatemala, Belize, and Honduras. They still try to keep some of their cultural traditions alive, but don't worry, they definitely do *not* practice bloodletting any more. And it's probably safe to play soccer with them, but make sure you win just in case!

Mexico Book List

From the Alamo to Day of the Dead celebrations, to Mexican pro wrestlers, plus the famous Mexican artists Diego Rivera and Frida Kahlo, you will find Mexico's proud cultural heritage represented in the books that follow.

Fiction

Ⓨ Farmer, Nancy. *The House of the Scorpion* (Atheneum, 2004) 400p. **IL** 6–9 **RL** 6.1. National Book Award, Newbery Honor, Printz Honor
    In this science fiction novel that takes place in futuristic Mexico, Matteo, a clone of the drug lord, El Patron, struggles with the reality that he shares DNA with one of the most evil men on Earth.

Fine, Edith Hope, and Judith Pinkerton Josephson. *Armando and the Blue Tarp School.* Illus. Hernan Sosa (Lee & Low, 2007) 32p. **IL** K–4 **RL** 2.7
    This picture book is based on the true story of Armando, who is too poor to go to school. He spends his days in Tijuana, Mexico, trash-picking at the garbage dump. But when Señor David sets down a blue tarp near the garbage dump and calls it "school," Armando starts attending classes.

Fleischman, Sid. *The Dream Stealer.* Illus. Peter Sís (Greenwillow, 2009) 96p. **IL** 3–5 **RL** 3.4

    A Mexican girl has strange adventures as she goes to the castle of the Dream Stealer to try to recover the dream he stole from her.

Fleischman, Sid. *The Giant Rat of Sumatra: or Pirates Galore.* Illus. John Hendrix (Greenwillow, 2005) 194p. **IL** 3–6 **RL** 5.1

    A pirate ship harbors in Mexican California in 1846 as war breaks out between the United States and Mexico.

Garza, Xavier. *Lucha Libre, The Man in the Silver Mask: A Bilingual Cuenta.* Trans. Luis Humberto Crosthwaite (Cinqo Puntos, 2005) **IL** 3–5 **RL** 9

    Carlitos attends a wrestling match in Mexico City with his father and notices that his favorite masked wrestler has eyes that are strangely familiar.

Keep, Richard Clemenson. *Clatter Bash! A Day of the Dead Celebration* (Peachtree, 2004) 32p. **IL** K–4 **RL** 2

    This rhyming picture book shows the traditions that celebrate the Day of the Dead.

Leavitt, Amie Jane. *The Alamo: An Interactive History Adventure* (Capstone, 2007) 112p. **IL** 3–6 **RL** 3.5

    This choose-your-own-adventure book allows children to study the Battle of the Alamo from the perspective of a Texan and a Mexican.

♟ Perez, Amada Irma. *My Diary from Here to There.* Illus. Maya Christina Gonzalez (Children's Book Press, 2002) 32p. **IL** 2–5 **RL** 3.4. Pura Belpré Honor

    This picture book describes the feelings of a young girl when her father decides to leave Mexico to look for work in the United States.

Resau, Laura. *What the Moon Saw* (Delacorte, 2006) 272p. **IL** 5–9 **RL** 6.6

    Fourteen-year-old Clara is invited to Mexico to meet her grandparents for the first time. When she gets there, she's stunned by their life: they live in a simple shack in a small mountain village, very different from suburban Maryland. But Clara loves it and starts to feel right at home.

♥ **Ryan, Pam Muñoz.** *Esperanza Rising* (Scholastic, 2000) 262p. **IL** 4–7 **RL** 5.5. Pura Belpré Medal

Esperanza and her mother are forced to leave their rich, fancy life in Mexico to go work as poor laborers in Southern California.

Salter, Sydney. *Jungle Crossing* (Harcourt, 2009) 215p. **IL** 4–7 **RL** 4.6

Kat would much rather spend her vacation with her friends at home than go on a family vacation to Mexico. Her chance at popularity will be ruined if she misses Fiona's "mini-camp," but while in Mexico, she learns that some things are more important than being in the popular crowd.

Scieszka, Jon. *Me Oh Maya!* Illus. Adam McCauley (Viking, 2003) 69p. **IL** 3–5 **RL** 4.1

Three modern-day kids are transported back in time to the main ring-ball court in Chichin Itza, Mexico, in 1000 C.E., where they must play for their lives against a Mayan High Priest.

Nonfiction

♥ **Bernier-Grand, Carmen T.** *Diego: Bigger than Life.* Illus. David Diaz (Marshall Cavendish, 2009) 64p. **IL** 6–9 **RL** 5.3. Pura Belpré Honor

Pictures and poems depict the life of Mexican artist Diego Rivera.

Garland, Sherry. *Voices of the Alamo.* Illus. Ronald Himler (Scholastic, 2000) 40p. **IL** 3–6 **RL** 6.3

The Alamo is in San Antonio, Texas, which is a part of the United States now, but this book traces its history back through time when it was a Spanish mission in Mexico.

Kops, Deborah. *Palenque* (Twenty-First Century, 2008) 80p. **IL** 4–8 **RL** 5.5

The ancient Mayan city called Palenque was buried in the jungle for hundreds of years until archaeologists began to uncover its buildings.

Lourie, Peter. *Hidden World of the Aztec* (Boyds Mills, 2006) 48 p. **IL** 4–7 **RL** 6

This book describes the archaeological digs in Mexico City that revealed the ancient Aztec city, Tenochtitlan.

Marín, Guadelupe Rivera. *My Papa Diego and Me: Memories of My Father and His Art* (Children's Book Press, 2009) 32p. **IL** 2–5 **RL** 5.2

Thirteen of Diego Rivera's paintings are paired with first-person text written by his daughter in Spanish and English.

Grades 7 and Up—Fiction

Landman, Tanya. *The Goldsmith's Daughter* (Candlewick, 2009) 283p. **IL** YA **RL** 5.5

The life of an Aztec girl is turned upside down when she falls in love with a Spanish foreigner who arrives in her city of Tenochtitlan.

Grades 7 and Up—Nonfiction

♥ Bernier-Grand, Carmen T. *Frida: Viva la Vida! (Long Live Life!)* (Marshall Cavendish, 2007) 64p. **IL** YA **RL** 4. Pura Belpré Honor

The difficult life of Mexican painter Frida Kahlo is depicted in first-person poems and in Kahlo's paintings themselves.

Caribbean Booktalks

Cuba, Jamaica, Dominican Republic, and Haiti are a few of the islands in the Caribbean Sea between North and South America. First "discovered" by Christopher Columbus in 1492 and colonized by Spain, the area became a hotbed for lawlessness when England started hiring privateers to terrorize Spanish ships and ports during the eighteenth century. As a stop on the slave trade from West Africa, slavery was a very real part of Caribbean history, and these islands are now home to a large African-Caribbean population. Students may be familiar with some islands in the Caribbean as vacation spots or from the Pirates of the Caribbean movies, but putting them in the context of this history will make learning about them even more exciting.

Fiction

Babbitt, Natalie. *Jack Plank Tells Tales* (Scholastic, 2007) 130p. **Jamaica. IL** 3–6 **RL** 5.2

Jack Plank is a former pirate . . . well, rejected pirate really. He was kicked off his pirate ship because he wasn't any good at plundering. So now he's a landlubber in a small Jamaican town, and he has no idea what to do with his life. So he sits around talking to his new neighbors and telling them stories about trolls, mermaids, buried treasure, a crocodile charmer, a haunted mummy's hand—all crazy but true stories from his days on the pirate ship. If you like funny books and really outrageous unbelievable stories, then you will love this book!

Danticat, Edwidge. *Anacaona, Golden Flower: Haiti, 1490* (Scholastic, 2005) 186p. **Haiti.** **IL** 4–7 **RL** 5.9

Anacaona is a member of the Taíno tribe in what is now modern Haiti. Her uncle is the chief, so either Anacaona or her brother Behechio will one day replace him as ruler of the tribe. Anacaona is worried that they will argue over who will get to be the next chief, but her worries are solved when she falls in love with Caonabo, the chief from another village. She decides to marry him and leave her own village to Behechio's rule. In 1491, they have their first baby, but, if you know your history, you know that their world is about to change drastically in 1492, when Spanish conquistadors land on the island. At first the Taíno think they are spirits who have come to haunt them. Their skin is so pale they can't be human. But the white men just start grabbing at all the gold they see around them, and when a servant tries to run away to safety with Anacaona's baby, the white men shoot their lightning sticks at her. Now Anacaona and her husband know that these men are not spirits but enemies who must be killed no matter what.

Danticat, Edwidge. *Behind the Mountains* (Scholastic, 2002) 166p. **Haiti.** **IL** 5–8 **RL** 6.3

The year is 1990 and thirteen-year-old Celiane lives in Haiti with her mother and older brother. Her father went to America because there were no jobs in Haiti. He sends the family money every month, but Celiane really can't wait for the day when he says that they can come live with him in New York. Meanwhile, she is happy enough living in the beautiful mountains of her home country. But in the capital city Port-au-Prince, people are protesting the upcoming election, using terror and violence to intimidate others into supporting their political party. When Celiane goes to visit her aunt in the city, she experiences the violence firsthand in a bomb attack on the street. She and her mother are both hurt in the attack and are now more determined than ever to go to America, but how will they get there? And once they are there, will life be any better?

Y Engle, Margarita. *The Surrender Tree: Poems of Cuba's Struggle for Freedom* (Henry Holt, 2008) 169p. **Cuba.** **IL** 5–8 **RL** 5.2. Newbery Honor, Pura Belpré Medal, Jane Addams Award

If you knew the plants and herbs that could heal people in the jungle, would you only heal the people you liked, or would you use your power to make life better for everyone? This is the question Rosa, a slave girl, must face in this book. Some people think she is a witch because she knows how to heal people, but there is nothing magical about her ability. When Cuban plantation owners declare war against Spain, the slaves are caught in the middle. They are freed from the plantation, but their freedom is illegal according to the Spanish rulers, so they still have to hide from slave hunters. Rosa goes into hiding, but for ten years of war she devotes her life to healing the wounded people she finds in the jungle. One day she finds an injured slave hunter named Lieutenant Death. Will she help him, even knowing that he may someday try to capture or kill her? Would you? Rosa was an actual person, and this book is based on actual events in Cuban history.

Engle, Margarita. *Tropical Secrets: Holocaust Refugees in Cuba* (Henry Holt, 2009) 199p. **Cuba. IL** 5–8 **RL** 9.6

In 1939, Jewish refugees fled from the Nazis in Europe, boarding ships to the United States. They didn't know if the United States would let them into the country or if they would be sent away back to Germany, but they had no other hope. They had to leave, and they would go to any country that would take them in. Daniel's parents only had enough money for one ticket, so they sent him alone and promised to come find him in New York when they could. But Daniel's ship was not allowed to enter New York, and now he is in Cuba, the only place that would let the refugees in. Yet even in Cuba, there is anti-Semitism. Daniel lives in a refugee camp with the other Jews, and there he becomes friends with a Cuban volunteer named Paloma who helps the refugees behind her father's back. Her father is a greedy businessman who would be furious if he knew what she was doing. This book is based on the true story of Jewish refugees who were turned away when they tried to enter the United States but were allowed to enter Cuba and start new lives there.

Nonfiction

Hamilton, Sue. *Henry Morgan* (Abdo, 2007) 32p. **Jamaica. IL** 4–7 **RL** 6.5

The 1600s were the golden age of piracy in the Caribbean. In Jamaica, the most feared buccaneer was Henry Morgan, known all over the Caribbean for his ruthless torture and plundering. He was so rich and powerful that there is a whole valley named after him in Jamaica where he became lieutenant governor. Wait, a pirate was one of the leaders of Jamaica? Well, sort of. See Morgan didn't consider himself a pirate at all, and in England, he was considered a hero. England and Spain were at war, and as an Englishman, he was acting under orders when he did all those dastardly deeds against Spanish ships and settlements. This book describes his most infamous raids, his brutal methods of torture, and his sneaky devious methods of warfare. He definitely did not fight fair. But was he a pirate or a hero? Read this book and decide for yourself.

Malam, John. *You Wouldn't Want to Be a Pirate's Prisoner! Horrible Things You'd Rather Not Know.* Illus. David Antram (Franklin Watts, 2002) 32p. **IL** 4–7 **RL** 4.7

> *Pirates of the Caribbean* is not just a movie. In the early eighteenth century, England and Holland were at war with Spain, so sea captains had permission from their governments to attack Spanish ships and plunder all their gold and valuables. These sailors were called privateers. It was a dangerous job, but they got really rich doing it. Once the war was over, they were supposed to stop, but some privateers wanted to keep on plundering for themselves, so they became pirates—the outlaws of the sea. The subtitle of this book is "Horrible Things You'd Rather Not Know," and the author means it. This book tells all the gruesome, bloody, and disgusting ways that pirates tortured their prisoners, so if you think that might be too much for you to handle, don't read this book. On the other hand, if you're curious about flogging, water torture, human barbeque, and other methods of torture, plus diseases that make you vomit black blood and die, then this book is for you.

Caribbean Book List

Headlines from more recent years tell of refugees risking their lives to flee harsh dictatorships and poverty. In this book list, you will find some memoirs of survival as well as a true story of local hero Bob Marley, who rose up from poverty to become an ambassador for peace and justice in Jamaica.

Fiction

Y Alvarez, Julia. *Before We Were Free* (Knopf, 2002) 167p. **Dominican Republic.** **IL** 5–8 **RL** 6.5. Pura Belpré Medal

> Twelve-year-old Anita lives in the Dominican Republic, which is ruled by a terrible dictator. Most of her extended family has immigrated to freedom in the United States, but Anita's family stays and is subject to house arrest and worse by the secret police. This story is based on the actual events of the author's cousin who stayed in the Dominican Republic after Alvarez left for the United States with her family.

Danticat, Edwidge. *Eight Days: A Story of Haiti.* Illus. Alix Delinois (Scholastic, 2010) 32p. **Haiti.** 🔲 3–6

This story of a boy who is trapped for eight days in the rubble after an earthquake will help readers understand the recent tragedy in Haiti.

Engle, Margarita. *Firefly Letters: A Suffragette's Journey to Cuba* (Henry Holt, 2010) 160p. **Cuba.** 🔲 6–9 🔳 11.7

Three alternating free-verse narratives tell the stories of three women in Cuba, one a slave, one a rich Cuban, and one a suffragette visiting from Sweden.

Hanson, Regina. *A Season for Mangoes.* Illus. Eric Velasquez (Clarion, 2004) 32p. **Jamaica.** 🔲 K–4 🔳 4.3

Sareen describes her experiences at her first all-night "sit-up," a Jamaican custom for mourning dead loved ones.

Higson, Charlie. *Hurricane Gold: A James Bond Adventure* (Hyperion, 2009) 364p. 🔲 4–7 🔳 5

In the 1930s, James Bond was still a teenager, but his adventures were already starting. In this book, he travels to Lagrimas Negras, a fictional Caribbean island, to try to rescue two American children abducted by criminals. See also the other books in the James Bond Adventure series.

Joseph, Lynn. *The Color of My Words* (Joanna Cotler, 2000) 138p. **Dominican Republic.** 🔲 4–7 🔳 5.5

Twelve-year-old Ana Rosa wants to be a writer, but that is a dangerous profession in the Dominican Republic where soldiers can kill you for speaking out against the government. On her thirteenth birthday, Ana Rosa learns tragically just how dangerous it is.

🏆 Landowne, Youme. *Sélavi, That Is Life: A Haitian Story of Hope* (Cinqo Puntos, 2004) 32p. **Haiti.** 🔲 1–4 🔳 3.5. Jane Addams Award

A homeless Haitian boy joins other street children, and together they build a home where they can take care of themselves and other homeless children.

Lawrence, Iain. *The Buccaneers* (Delacorte, 2001) 244p. 🔲 5–8 🔳 5.9

In the eighteenth century, sixteen-year-old John encounters pirates, fierce storms, fever, and a strange man who may be cursed, as he sails his merchant ship from England to the Caribbean. See also the other books in the <u>High Seas Trilogy</u>.

Mordecai, Martin. *Blue Mountain Trouble* (Scholastic, 2009) 353p. **Jamaica.**
IL 5–7 **RL** 5.6

 Twelve-year-old twins living in the mountains in Jamaica have to deal with their mother getting sick and with the local jailbird making trouble for them.

Veciana-Suarez, Ana. *Flight to Freedom* (Scholastic, 2002) 215p. **Cuba. IL**
6–8 **RL** 6.2

 In 1967, the Communist regime in Cuba under Fidel Castro makes life so horrible for thirteen-year-old Yara and her family that they try to find a way to immigrate to Miami.

Nonfiction

Cherry, Lynne. *The Sea, the Storm and the Mangrove Tangle* (FSG, 2004)
32p. **IL** K–4 **RL** 4.4

 This picture book shows how a mangrove seed grows into a forest that will shelter birds and animals even during a hurricane.

Medina, Tony. *I and I: Bob Marley.* Illus. Jesse Joshua Watson (Lee & Low, 2009) 40p. **Jamaica. IL** 4–8 **RL** 3.4

 This picture book biography of musician Bob Marley shows how his childhood in "Trenchtown" influenced his music.

Grades 7 and Up—Fiction

Rees, Celia. *Pirates!: The True and Remarkable Adventures of Minerva Sharpe and Nancy Kington, Female Pirates* (Bloomsbury, 2003) 340p. **Jamaica. IL** YA **RL** 6.9

 Nancy Kington, daughter of a rich merchant, suddenly orphaned when her father dies, is sent to live on her family's plantation in Jamaica. Disgusted by the treatment of the slaves and her brother's willingness to marry her off, she and one of the slaves, Minerva, run away and join a band of pirates.

Grades 7 and Up—Nonfiction

🏆 **Engle, Margarita.** *Poet Slave of Cuba: Biography of Juan Francisco Manzano.* Illus. Sean Qualls (Henry Holt, 2006) 183p. **Cuba.** **IL** YA **RL** 5.5. Pura Belpré Medal

    This biography is told in verse from the perspectives of several people in Juan's life and describes the harsh conditions of Cuban slaves in the 1800s.

Chapter 6

Australia, New Zealand, and South Pacific Islands

Even though it is the world's smallest continent, Australia is home to some very strange animals, some of which are not found anywhere else in the world. Its aboriginal history is also fascinating, as is the initial meeting of the native South Pacific Islanders with the first European they ever saw, Captain James Cook. Obviously, this meeting has had profound and lasting effects on the natives' lives.

Australia, New Zealand, and South Pacific Islands Booktalks

Fiction

Clarke, Judith. *Kalpana's Dream* (Front Street, 2004) 164p. **Australia.** 🄻 6–9 🆁🄻 5.5

If you like books that have a sort of mysterious randomness to them, then you will like this book. On Neema's first day at her new upper school, which is probably like our eighth grade, she meets a new boy named Gull who looks so familiar, she thinks she must have met him somewhere before but doesn't know where. He feels the same tingly recognition, so he starts riding his skateboard past her house every night, hoping he'll see her again. He doesn't see Neema, but he does see her great-grandmother, Kalpana, who is visiting from India and doesn't speak any English. Kalpana's dream is to fly, so when she sees Gull on his skateboard, she is fascinated and calls him Flying Boy. Meanwhile, there are rumors around school that Neema's English teacher, Ms. Dallimore, is dating a vampire. He picks her up every day in a hearse-like black car. He always wears dark sunglasses, and Ms. Dallimore is getting paler by the day. All of these plotlines come together in the end when Neema and Gull finally find each other, Kalpana gets to fly, and you find out once and for all what's going on with Ms. Dallimore's boyfriend. I'm warning you, the ending of this book is completely random. You might like it, or you might hate it, but it will definitely make you think!

Cowley, Joy. *Hunter* (Philomel, 2004) 153p. **New Zealand.** 🔳 5–8 🔳 4

The year is 1805, and Hunter is a Maori slave in the tribe that kidnapped him when he was very young. He is badly treated and has no rights or freedom of any kind, but he is respected in one way: he has the gift of Tane that allows him to see visions of things before they happen. So the tribe members rely on him on their hunting expeditions to sense where the animals are. Without him, the tribe would have a much harder time surviving. Lately, though, Hunter keeps having new visions that he can't figure out. They feature a pale white girl who falls out of a giant metal bird from the sky. He doesn't know who she is, but he knows he needs to help her somehow. Meanwhile, in 2005, Jordan and her brothers are getting on a plane to go home for the holidays. And here is the freaky part: their plane is about to crash over a small island in New Zealand, and Jordan and Hunter's worlds are about to come together.

Falkner, Brian. *The Tomorrow Code* (Random House, 2008) 368p. **New Zealand.** 🔳 6–9 🔳 5

This book starts a little slow, but be patient; it gets really good! Tane and his best friend Rebecca are wondering whether time travel is possible. Rebecca's parents are both prominent scientists in New Zealand, so she knows it's not possible to actually move yourself to a different time. But she does think it's possible to send messages through time. Rebecca thinks if they could get the raw data from gamma ray bursts in space, they could put them into binary code and look for patterns that might be a message from the future. It's a long shot, but maybe someone is sending them a message right now! To their surprise, it actually works. They find a pattern and figure out that the message is in Morse code. It's a lottery number from the future, so they play it—and win a huge jackpot! But when they decode the rest of the message, they get the shock of their lives. It's an SOS . . . from themselves in the future. From this point on, the book explodes with action. A biological disaster is about to destroy all the humans on Earth, and Rebecca and Tane have sent themselves a warning with instructions for how to prevent the catastrophe, but can they decode it in time?

Gleitzman, Morris. *Toad Away* (Random House, 2006) 208p. **Australia.** **IL** 3–6 **RL** 3.9

If you like hilarious, ridiculous, laugh-out-loud funny books, then you will love this one, but don't read it in public because you'll be falling off your chair laughing and people will think you're crazy. This is the story of Limpy, a cane toad who lives in Australia with his other cane toad relatives. But they have a big problem. Limpy's rellies (relatives) keep getting squashed flat by humans driving cars, and Limpy decides to do something about it. Limpy's dimwitted cousin Goliath wants to declare war on all humans by peeing in their food and spitting slime on them until they agree to stop killing the toads. But Limpy knows that violence is not the answer. Limpy thinks if he could just become friends with the humans, then they would learn respect and change their toad-squashing ways. This quest leads Limpy far away from his familiar swamp to exotic new places like a human supermarket, a human poo farm, and all the way to the Amazon jungle. You'll be laughing from beginning to end of this book! See also *Toad Rage* (Random House, 2004) and *Toad Heaven* (Random House, 2005).

▰ Video Booktalk: http://bookwink.com/archive_2009_03_28.html

Marshall, James Vance. *Stories from the Billabong.* Illus. Francis Firebrace (Frances Lincoln, 2008) 61p. **Australia.** **IL** 2–6 **RL** 4.6

Have you ever wondered how the kangaroo got its pouch? Or how the crocodile got its scales? Or why frogs can only croak? The stories in this book are more than 10,000 years old and were told by the Aboriginal people of Australia. They describe the events of the "Dreamtime," when they believe Earth and all its creatures were created. Each story describes ancient beliefs about a plant or animal native to Australia and follows with a page of facts so that you can compare the ancient ideas with modern scientific ideas. The illustrations were all painted by a member of an Aboriginal tribe, so you really feel like you're experiencing the stories the way they were told thousands of years ago!

Nonfiction

Bishop, Nic. *Nic Bishop Marsupials* (Scholastic, 2009) 48p. **Australia.** **IL** 2–6 **RL** 7.4

The first sentence of this book reads, "Most people know about lions, zebras, monkeys and bears, but what about bettongs and bilbies? Or potoroos and pademelons? Dibblers and dunnarts?" I love it already because it's going to be about something called a dibbler! Then the book just goes on to knock my socks off! Every page is an amazing picture and description of some wacky animal that lives in Australia and carries its babies around in a pouch. The kangaroo is the most well-known marsupial, but there are lots of others that you've probably never heard of or seen a close-up picture of! The wombat, the numbat, the quoll, and the Tasmanian devil in all their glory appear in this book. You will also see the smallest marsupial in the world, the planigale, which is only two inches long but will attack a cockroach or a spider as big as it is with the same ferocity that a lion attacks a zebra. At the end of the book, Nic Bishop describes how he captured all these animals on film, how he had to wait for hours lying on his belly for a wombat to turn and look at the camera. He also describes how he used a camera trap at night to capture the nocturnal animals. He put an invisible trigger beam of infrared light where he thought the animals would show up at night, and he would leave food to attract them, too. When they crossed the light, it triggered the camera to take a picture automatically. Then in the morning, he would look and see what animals he had "caught." There is a cute shot of some possums eating the midnight snack Nic Bishop left for them!

Collard, Sneed B. *One Night in the Coral Sea.* Illus. Robin Brickman (Charlesbridge, 2005) 32p. **Australia.** **IL** 3–5 **RL** 5

To spawn means to produce lots and lots of young at one time. Like in scary science fiction movies where the alien spawn takes over Earth. Well, this picture book describes how corals spawn, and it's really cool. On Australia's Great Barrier Reef, one night in springtime every year, an amazing spectacle takes place. Each coral produces a polyp, a little packet of eggs, and then the polyp pops open and all the eggs are released into the ocean. Imagine trillions of brightly colored tiny eggs floating around the surface of the ocean! This book describes what happens to all those eggs on their journey to becoming adult corals.

Collard, Sneed B. *A Platypus, Probably.* Illus. Andrew Plant (Charlesbridge, 2005) 32p. **Australia.** ■ K–4 ■ 3.2

The platypus has got to be one of the strangest mammals on earth. It was around during the time of the dinosaurs and still exists today, but it only lives in Australia. There is nowhere else you can ever see one in the wild. It looks like it's half duck, half beaver. It has webbed feet and a big bill like a duck. But it has fur and a wide, flat tail like a beaver. It sleeps in an underground burrow during the day and hunts for food on the river bottom at night. And here is the really weird thing: it lays eggs. OK, birds lay eggs and fish lay eggs, and spiders lay eggs, but how many mammals have you heard of that lay eggs? Weird, I know, but this book has some really cute pictures of the babies when they hatch. If you are interested in rare animals, take a look at this picture book.

Lawlor, Laurie. *Magnificent Voyage: An American Adventurer on Captain James Cook's Final Expedition* (Holiday House, 2002) 236p. **Polynesia.** ■ 6–9 ■ 7.1

By 1776, Captain Cook was a celebrity. He was the first European explorer to visit the Pacific Islands. He was the first white person the natives of Tahiti and New Zealand had ever seen. This book describes the true story of Cook's third and final voyage in the Pacific. His goal was to find a Northwest Passage—a seaway through North America that would connect the Pacific and Atlantic Oceans. No one had charted the west coast of North America before, so they thought there might be an opening that would take sailors all the way across the country to the Atlantic coast. But even though Cook was an experienced explorer and a national hero in England, he made serious mistakes and miscalculations on this trip that caused it to go disastrously wrong, so much so that Cook himself ended up getting killed by angry natives in Hawaii. The ship leaked from the beginning. There were weather delays that caused them to burn through their food and fresh water faster than they planned. But worst of all were the fights with the natives. How could such an expert captain run such a disastrous voyage? What did he do to make the natives so angry that they killed him? Read this book to find out.

🏆 Montgomery, Sy. *The Quest for the Tree Kangaroo: An Expedition to the Cloud Forest of New Guinea.* Photog. Nic Bishop (Houghton Mifflin, 2006) 80p. **Papua New Guinea.** ■ 4–9 ■ 6.2. Sibert Honor

This book is about a scientist who traveled to Papua New Guinea to study the Matschie's tree kangaroo. It describes her grueling three-day hike into the cloud forest, a tropical forest so high in the mountains, it's in the clouds. For nine hours a day, she and her crew hiked through mud, rain, and blood-sucking leeches up where the air was so thin they could hardly breathe. When they finally got to their camp, they started looking for the tree kangaroo. This book describes everything the scientists had to do, from tracking and capturing the animals, to examining them, to learning to speak with the natives and packing enough toilet paper! If you're interested in studying animals in the wild, this is a great book.

◢Video Booktalk: http://www.bookwink.com/archive_2008_10_13.html

Australia, New Zealand, and South Pacific Islands Book List

Although the animals and environment may be very different, kids reading contemporary stories in this book list will discover that, even though it is really far away, the lives of kids and teens in Australia and New Zealand are not much different from those in Western countries of the world.

Fiction

French, Simon. *Where in the World* (Peachtree, 2003) 174p. **Australia.** ⬛ 5–8 ▦ 4.3

> Ari moves from Germany to Australia with his mother and must learn a new language and get used to a new school and people. Playing the violin is the one thing that makes him feel at home.

Lawrence, Iain. *The Cannibals* (Delacorte, 2005) 240p. **South Pacific Islands.** ⬛ 6–9 ▦ 5.2

> Tom Tin is wrongly accused of murder and sent away on a convict ship to Australia, but he makes plans to escape with Midgeley, another innocent convict. See also *The Convicts* (Delacorte, 2004) and *The Castaways* (Delacorte, 2007).

Nonfiction

Arnold, Caroline. *Uluru: Australia's Aboriginal Heart.* Photog. Arthur Arnold (Clarion, 2003) 64p. **Australia.** ⬛ 5–8 ▦ 7

> In the middle of Australia in Uluru-Kata Tjuta National Park sits the world's largest single rock. More than a thousand feet high, this rock,

called Uluru, is sacred to the native people, who told stories about the creation of the land and people.

Banting, Erinn. *The Great Barrier Reef* (Weigl, 2005) 32p. **Australia.** ■ 4–7 **RL** 6

Learn all about the largest coral reef in the world with this picture book.

Markle, Sandra. *Finding Home.* Illus. Alan Marks (Charlesbridge, 2008) 32p. **Australia.** ■ K–4 **RL** 6.4

When a koala's home is destroyed by a bushfire, it wanders twelve miles away into the dangerous human suburb, even crossing a busy highway, to find a new home. This picture book is based on a true story.

Markle, Sandra. *Hip-Pocket Papa.* Illus. Alan Marks (Charlesbridge, 2010) 32p. **Australia.** ■ K–4 **RL** 9.5

When the tadpoles of the miniature hip-pocket frog hatch, they climb into pouches on the father's legs. He then carries them across the dangerous forest floor to water. This picture book illustrates the process from beginning to happy ending.

Montgomery, Sy. *Kakapo Rescue: Saving the World's Strangest Parrot.* Photog. Nic Bishop (Houghton Mifflin, 2010) 80p. **New Zealand.** ■ 4-8 **RL** 7.4

This book describes how people are working to protect this endangered nocturnal bird that lives in underground nests in New Zealand.

O'Brien, Patrick. *The Mutiny on the Bounty* (Walker, 2007) 40p. **Polynesia.** ■ 3–7 **RL** 5.7

This picture book depicts the true story of the crew of the ship *Bounty* that sailed from England to Tahiti in 1788 and how they rebelled against the captain, a crime punishable by death.

Grades 7 and Up—Fiction

♈ **Clarke, Judith.** *One Whole and Perfect Day* (Front Street, 2007) 248p. **Australia.** ■ YA **RL** 5. Printz Honor

Sensible teenager Lily learns how to deal with her embarrassment about her eccentric family when they all come together for a party.

♕ **Marchetta, Melina.** *Jellicoe Road* (HarperTeen, 2006) 420p. **Australia.** 🆔
YA 🆁🄻 4.8. Printz Award

Seventeen-year-old Taylor, a dorm leader at her boarding school in Australia, tries to figure out the mystery of her past when her mother abandoned her.

Moriarty, Jaclyn. *Feeling Sorry for Celia* (St. Martins Griffin, 2002) 288p.
Australia. 🆔 YA 🆁🄻 7.1

Readers get to know high school student Elizabeth through letters from her and to her from the various people in her life, including her flighty best friend Celia. See also the companion novels *The Year of Secret Assignments* (Scholastic, 2004), *Murder of Bindy Mackenzie* (Scholastic, 2006), and *The Ghosts of Ashbury High* (Scholastic, 2010).

Moriarty, Jaclyn. *The Spell Book of Listen Taylor* (Scholastic, 2007) 496p.
Australia. 🆔 YA 🆁🄻 5

Alissa (Listen) Taylor becomes embroiled in the Zing family secret when she discovers a spell book and, not thinking the spells are real, starts performing them.

Chapter 7

Arctic and Antarctica

No humans live in Antarctica (the South Pole), although there are research stations where scientists can live for a few months while they study the animals and environment. In 1773, Captain James Cook almost sailed to Antarctica, but the treacherous conditions forced him to turn back. This started a dangerous race among explorers to be the first to get to Antarctica. Every single story is nail-bitingly exciting! The stories of modern scientists in Antarctica, although not as dangerous, are interesting in their own way, especially for kids who are interested in marine biology, meteorology, and geology—or kids who love penguins. The race to the North Pole was just as thrilling, but maybe slightly less dangerous, because the Arctic was already populated with humans. The Inuit tribes who lived there helped explorers like Matthew Henson and Robert Peary, and taught them how to survive in the frozen north.

Arctic and Antarctica Booktalks

Fiction

Lerangis, Peter. *Antarctica: Journey to the Pole* (Scholastic, 2000) 242p. **IL** 4–7 **RL** 4.5

This is the fictional story of a secret expedition to discover the South Pole. The year is 1909, and several people have come close, but no one has traveled all the way to the bottom of the world yet. American Jack Winslow wants to be the first, but he has to keep it a secret because he doesn't want anyone else to beat him. But there are several problems. First he has to bring his sixteen-year-old son Colin and his fifteen-year-old stepson Andrew, who don't get along. At all. Second, he has to bring Philip the lazy, useless nephew of the millionaire who is backing the expedition. This would be bad enough on a Caribbean cruise, but on an expedition like this one where everyone's survival is at stake, you are only as strong as your weakest link. Needless to say, there are problems. Be warned, this books ends in a cliffhanger just as the ice is about to chop their ship in half, so you will want to have the sequel, *Antarctica: Escape from Disaster* (Scholastic, 2000), to find out what happens.

McKernan, Virginia. *Shackleton's Stowaway* (Random House, 2005) 336p. **IL** 5–9 **RL** 6.1

Desperate for an adventure, eighteen-year-old Perce Blackborrow stows away on board Shackleton's ship bound to explore the Antarctic continent. But everything that could go wrong, does go wrong. The ship becomes trapped as ice freezes around it, and then crushes it. The men evacuate onto the ice, but the ship sinks with no hope of rescue. If the men are going to survive in the most hostile place on earth, they will have to do it on their own. This book is based on the true story of the actual men who miraculously all survived—although there were a few close calls and an emergency frostbite surgery. To find out how they did it and how they finally made it home, read this book!

Nonfiction

Conlan, Kathy. *Under the Ice* (Kids Can Press, 2002) 56p. **IL** 4–8 **RL** 6

If you think walking around on land in Antarctica would be cold, imagine drilling a hole in the ice and going swimming! Even with the warmest wet suit in the world, can you think of anything worse? But that is exactly what the scientist featured in this book traveled to Antarctica to do. Her name is Kathy Conlan, and she is a marine biologist. This book is the true story of her scuba diving expedition to study the effects of ice scraping on the ocean floor. This book shows you everything she saw under the ice, including seals, penguins, and some strange looking plants on the ocean floor. If you're interested in marine biology, don't miss this book!

Dewey, Jennifer Owings. *Antarctic Journal: Four Months at the Bottom of the World* (HarperCollins, 2001) 64p. **IL** 3–6 **RL** 4.9

Did you know that penguins can die of heat stroke if it gets too warm, like above freezing? And in the summer, the sun in Antarctica is so strong that you can get a blistering sunburn if you don't wear sunscreen? Today the entire continent of Antarctica is a "world park." No humans are allowed to live there permanently, but scientists may visit to study the land and wildlife. There is a dormitory set up where they can live and work. This book describes the experiences of one artist who spent four months in Antarctica with visiting scientists from all over the world. She spent the time exploring and drawing the animals and scenery she saw. She describes how strange it feels when the sun stays out all night long, what Christmas is like at the scientist station, and the day she spent watching the penguins and they came right up to her! She includes her sketches and drawings, so you feel like you are right there, seeing what she sees.

Farr, Richard. *Emperors of the Ice: A True Story of Disaster and Survival in the Antarctic, 1910–13* (FSG, 2008) 217p. **IL** 6–9 **RL** 7.8

After reading this book, I have two pieces of advice: 1) Don't read it without a warm blanket or a snuggie. You will be shivering just reading the descriptions of the freezing cold. 2) Don't go to Antarctica. Just kidding . . . Sort of. This is the true story of a group of men who planned to spend three years in Antarctica, studying the wildlife and making other scientific observations. The beginning of the book is a little boring. (They only almost die in the horrible stormy waters that circle the bottom of the world.) But once they arrive on Antarctica, then the book really gets exciting with vivid descriptions of painful frostbite, attacks by killer whales, and lots more narrow escapes from death. This book will make you so happy to be safe and warm at home, or if you're crazy, it will make you want to go exploring in Antarctica!

Johnson, Dolores. *Onward: A Photobiography of African-American Polar Explorer Matthew Henson* (National Geographic, 2005) 64p. **IL** 5–8 **RL** 6.4

In 1909, Admiral Robert E. Peary was honored by the National Geographic Society for being the first person to reach the North Pole. But it wasn't until 2000 that Matthew Henson, Peary's partner on all of his Arctic expeditions for twenty-three years, was given the same honor. Why did they not get the award at the same time? It was because Henson was African American, and people assumed he was just Peary's "manservant." Well, this book sets the record straight and tells the true story of how Henson helped Peary reach the North Pole. It describes how Peary's toes snapped off from frostbite, and Henson carried him for eleven days back to camp. After you read this book, it should be obvious that without Henson, Peary never would have reached the Pole—and might not have even survived. He never could have done it without Matthew Henson.

Kirkpatrick, Katherine. *The Snow Baby: The Arctic Childhood of Admiral Robert E. Peary's Daring Daughter* (Holiday House, 2007) 50p. **IL** 4–8 **RL** 7.8

Marie Peary's birth in 1893 was newsworthy for two reasons: first, she was the child of the famous arctic explorer Robert E. Peary, who was trying to be the first person to reach the North Pole, and second, she was an American born among the Inuit in the freezing cold far north of Greenland. The Inuit had never seen a baby so white before, and they called her Snow Baby because they thought she was made of snow! This is the story of her unusual childhood in the Arctic wilderness, how she had to dress in animal furs to keep warm, how she played with Inuit children and learned their language, and how her father finally reached the North Pole.

Myers, Walter Dean. *Antarctica: Journeys to the South Pole* (Scholastic, 2004) 134p. **IL** 6–9 **RL** 8.6

Imagine flying to Mars in a rocket made of tin cans. That's kind of what it was like for the first explorers to travel in the Antarctic Circle. They had no idea what they would find. They didn't have proper clothes to protect them from the brutal cold. They had never experienced cold like that before! They had no map because no one had ever been there before to make one. They didn't know if there would be strange new people or animals there. But the most dangerous unknown was the ice. There was lots of ice floating around and poking up out of the water. It might not look dangerous, but it was sharp. If the wooden ships hit it, the ice could break a hole right through them. Not only that, if the temperature dropped low enough, the ocean could freeze solid, trapping them in the ice for months. What kind of crazy person would volunteer for a journey like that? Well, this book tells you all about the first brave explorers to attempt this insane trip and everything that happened to them along the way.

🏆 **Webb, Sophie.** *My Season with Penguins: An Antarctic Journal* (Houghton Mifflin, 2000) 48p. 🅸🅻 4–7 🆁🅻 6.9. Sibert Honor

This book answers some important questions about living in Antarctica. For example, what color is penguin poop? The answer might surprise you! And one other fact about poop you'll learn from this book: it's too cold for poop to decompose there, so humans who make any have to bring it back with them when they leave Antarctica! Think about that for a second. EWW! This book is the true diary of a woman who lived in Antarctica for two months to study the Adelie penguins that live there. It's full of fascinating facts about the adorable little Adelie penguin, smaller cousin to the giant Emperor penguin, and it also gives you a good idea of what life is like for wildlife scientists working in the freezing cold.

Arctic and Antarctica Book List

Where Arctic and Antarctic exploration are concerned, truth is definitely stranger than fiction. The explorers are characters in themselves, and their true adventures are every bit as exciting as any made-up story. This list includes biographies of Ernest Shackleton and Matthew Henson, just two of the brave men who risked their lives (not to mention their fingers and toes) to find the furthest reaches of Earth.

Nonfiction

Armstrong, Jennifer. *Shipwreck at the Bottom of the World: The Extraordinary True Story of Shackleton and the Endurance* (Crown, 1998) 134p. 🅸🅻 6–9 🆁🅻 6.5

The true story of the twenty-eight men who were stranded in the most hostile place on earth, and all of them survived.

Arnold, Caroline. *Global Warming and the Dinosaurs: Fossil Discoveries at the Poles.* Illus. Laurie Caple (Clarion, 2009) 40p. 🅸🅻 3–6 🆁🅻 4

In contrast to the popular depictions of dinosaurs living in tropical climates, this book describes evidence of dinosaurs who lived at the North and South Poles.

Bledsoe, Lucy Jane. *How to Survive in Antarctica* (Holiday House, 2006) 101p. **IL** 4–8 **RL** 5

 Based on her several trips to Antarctica, the author tells you everything you need to know to get ready to visit the South Pole.

Kimmel, Elizabeth Cody. *Ice Story: Shackleton's Lost Expedition* (Clarion, 1999) 120p. **IL** 4–8 **RL** 7.6

 With actual photographs from the expedition, this book tells and shows the story of Shackleton's failed attempt to cross Antarctica. Even though they failed, the entire crew miraculously survived.

Latta, Sara L. *Ice Scientist: Careers in the Frozen Antarctic* (Enslow, 2009) 128p. **IL** 5-8

 First person narratives from a variety of scientists show readers what it is like to work in Antarctica.

Markle, Sandra. *A Mother's Journey.* Illus. Alan Marks (Charlesbridge, 2005) 32p. **IL** K–4 **RL** 3.4

 This picture book follows the female Emperor penguin on her five-day journey across the ice in search of food, and then back again to the breeding grounds where her newly hatched chick waits for its first meal.

Ryan, Zoe Alderfer. *Ann and Liv Cross Antarctica: A Dream Come True.* Illus. Nicholas Reti (De Capo, 2001) 32p. **IL** 4–7

 This picture book is the true story of two women who, in 2000, attempted to cross Antarctica on foot, traveling 2,400 miles in 100 days.

Tatham, Betty. *Penguin Chick.* Illus. Helen K. Davie (HarperCollins, 2002) 33p. **IL** 2–4 **RL** 2.9

 A simple picture book story of the life cycle of a penguin chick, from egg to adulthood.

Weatherford, Carole Boston. *I, Matthew Henson: Polar Explorer.* Illus. Eric Velasquez (Walker, 2007) 32p. **IL** 2–4 **RL** 7.8

 This picture book biography uses first-person poems to describe Matthew Henson's life, including his exploration of the North Pole and the racism he experienced at home.

Chapter 8

Ancient Civilizations

Ancient Egypt Booktalks

The ancient Egyptian Empire was a civilization that thrived along the Nile River in northern Africa from about 3000 B.C.E. until the Roman conquest in 31 B.C.E. In 332 B.C.E., Egypt fell under the rule of the ancient Greek Empire, and Alexandria became its capital, but traditional Egyptian life stayed largely the same. In almost every other chapter of this book, it made sense to separate the books according to the geographical region as we currently define it, but this ancient Egypt section forced me to question that logic. Alexandria, for example, is geographically located in current-day Egypt, but a book about the great library in Alexandria would most likely describe the great thinkers of ancient Greece. So books about the Greek scholars who lived and worked in Alexandria—even Hypatia, who lived during the ancient Roman era—are listed in the ancient Greece section. I wasn't completely consistent in that logic, however. Cleopatra caused me some angst. She was a Greek princess living in Egypt at the cusp of the ancient Roman era. For simplicity's sake, I left her with the Egyptians. Her father was called the pharaoh, after all. The rest of the books in this section on ancient Egypt are what you would expect: pharaohs, pyramids, the sphinx, mummies, and the archaeologists who explore their fascinating mysteries.

Fiction

Friesner, Esther. *Sphinx's Princess* (Random House, 2009) 370p. **IL** 4–8 **RL** 5.4

Nefertiti's name means "the beautiful woman has come," and Nefertiti is very beautiful—but she's also smart. It's a good thing, too, because her father has enemies who would love to use her to get at his power, and "friends" who would love to use her for their own power. Through it all, Nefertiti just wants to live a normal life caring for the people she loves: her little sister and Berrett, a mute slave girl whose older sister was killed. But when the pharaoh's wife summons her to their palace and tells her that she has to marry her son, the future pharaoh, Nefertiti has no choice but to obey. This book gives you an idea of what it was like to live in a pharaoh's castle, but it's also a really good story about a girl who's just trying to protect herself in a dangerous political situation in which one false move could have her sentenced to death.

Gregory, Kristiana. *Cleopatra VII: Daughter of the Nile, 57 B.C.* (Scholastic, 1999) 221p. **IL** 4–8 **RL** 6.5

I know when you think of Cleopatra, you think queen of Egypt, not Greece. She was the queen of Egypt, but she was not a native Egyptian. Her family was Greek, and they ruled Egypt during the time of the Greek Empire. This book is a fictional diary of what her life might have been like back then. And if this diary is anything to go by, her life was not boring! In the first chapter, she finds out that someone is trying to kill her father, the pharaoh, and her whole family is in danger. Her life just gets worse after that as she travels with her father to Rome to beg for the Roman army's help in defeating his enemies. Rome is a barbaric place compared with their palace in Alexandria, Egypt, and the Romans at first insult Cleopatra and her father in Latin, thinking they can't understand their language. But Cleopatra does speak Latin, as well as several other languages, and even though she is only twelve years old, she totally puts those big old Romans in their place. She lived more than 2,000 years ago, but this diary makes her seem real and modern, as she struggles to deal with her alcoholic father, her conniving sisters, and adults who don't take her seriously because she is still a child.

Harvey, Gill. *Orphan of the Sun* (Bloomsbury, 2006) 310p. **IL** 5–9 **RL** 4.3

Meryt-Re is upset because she has just received a marriage proposal from Ramose and she doesn't want to marry him. Normally, it would be OK to refuse him, but since her parents died, she has been living with her aunt and uncle, and her uncle wants to get rid of her. Even worse is the rumor that Meryt may be under the power of Sekhmet, the goddess of destruction. If people believe that Meryt can curse people, then no one will ever want to marry her. Meryt doesn't want to curse anyone, but she does have strange dreams that predict the future. Is it possible that she has more power than she thinks? Meryt doesn't know what to do, but she is forced to make a decision when her cousin becomes deathly ill. It's true that Meryt hated him, but she never cursed him! Her uncle of course blames Meryt and kicks her out of the house. Now she has to figure out what to do with her life. Will she take the safe route and marry Ramose, even though she doesn't love him? Or will she face up to her own power and learn how to interpret her prophetic dreams?

Nonfiction

Andronik, Catherine M. *Hatshepsut, His Majesty, Herself.* Illus. Joseph Daniel Fiedler (Atheneum, 2001) 40p. **IL** 3–6 **RL** 7.3

In ancient Egypt, the pharaoh ruled the land and was considered a god. The pharaoh was always a man . . . or was he? In the 1920s, archaeologists made discoveries that pointed to a woman pharaoh, and her name was Hatshepsut. She was the pharaoh's daughter, and when he died, there were no sons to take his place, so Hatshepsut became the "regent" until her young nephew was old enough to be the real pharaoh. But Hatshepsut acted like she was pharaoh. She dressed like a man and even attached a false golden beard to her chin. She was actually such a good regent that she declared herself pharaoh, and the people accepted her rule for more than twenty years. Why, then, was she forgotten and only discovered again thousands of years later? Well, that little nephew finally did become pharaoh after her, but he was not at all happy about succeeding a woman king, so he tried to destroy all records of her.

Butcher, Kristin. *Pharaohs and Foot Soldiers: One Hundred Ancient Egyptian Jobs You Might Have Desired or Dreaded.* Illus. Martha Newbigger (Annick, 2009) 96p. **IL** 3–6 **RL** 6

You might not think that a book about ancient Egyptian jobs would be funny, but this is a comical look at what life was like for all classes of Egyptian society. It describes all the possible jobs you could have had if you lived back then. You could have been a soldier in the army, or a stone hauler for the huge monuments, or a sandal-bearer for the pharaoh. Or maybe you would have been a manicurist, or a tattoo artist, or a dream interpreter. Don't forget about the tomb jobs like mummy maker, cutter, or embalmer. And if you can't make an honest living, this book even tells you how to be an ancient Egyptian robber.

Giblin, James Cross. *Secrets of the Sphinx.* Illus. Bagram Ibatoulline (Scholastic, 2004) 48p. **IL** 4–9 **RL** 8.6

If you go to Egypt today, you can visit the Great Sphinx, a giant statue six stories high made of rock. It has the body of a lion and the head of the pharaoh Khafre, and it is meant to be a symbol of strength and power. Over the years, the statue has been damaged by erosion, had its face broken by vandals, and was actually buried under sand for hundreds of years before being rediscovered. This book describes how it was built, why it was built, and what it must have looked like in its original glory. It also tells the legend of Atlantis, the mysterious underwater civilization, and about a group of people today who believe that the lost records of Atlantis are buried under the Sphinx's paws. People actually tried to look for them, but they haven't found anything . . . yet.

Hawass, Zahi. *Curse of the Pharaohs: My Adventures with Mummies* (National Geographic, 2004) 144p. **IL** 4–8 **RL** 7

The ancient Egyptians buried their pharaohs with (literally) tons of valuable treasure because they believed that they would need it in the afterlife. But if robbers knew where the tomb was, they would go and steal the treasure for themselves. Apparently this was pretty common, so the Egyptians started burying the pharaohs in secret tombs hidden away from everyone. And as an extra precaution, they put curses on the tombs, so anyone who entered would have something terrible happen to them. The idea of the curse became famous in 1922 when the tomb of King Tutankhamun was discovered by Howard Carter and a team of British archaeologists. On the day they made the discovery, Carter came home and found a cobra eating his pet canary. Soon after, Lord Carnarvon, who funded the expedition, died of pneumonia. Since then, there have been many other stories of people who touched ancient Egyptian artifacts and then coincidentally had bad luck, got sick, or even died. But is it true that the tombs are really cursed? This book tells the stories of all the bad luck associated with the tombs and tries to figure out whether these things happened because of a curse or if there could be another explanation.

Pemberton, Delia. *Egyptian Mummies: People from the Past* (Harcourt, 2001) 48p. **IL** 3–6 **RL** 7

You have probably heard of mummies, those dead guys from ancient Egypt all wrapped up in bandages. Well this book answers every question you ever had about them. Like why did the Egyptians do that? How did they do it? How long does it take to become a mummy? Do they smell? Did they really stick a tool up the mummy's nose to scrape its brains out? Did they really scoop out the stomach and intestines and keep them in jars? Eww. Why? This book explains it all. It also explains the bizarre beliefs people have about mummies in modern times. Can swallowing ground-up powder of a mummy really cure diseases, or will it just make you throw up? If you enter a mummy's tomb, will you be cursed? Can mummies rise from the dead and kill you? This book answers all these important questions and more.

Weitzman, David. *Pharaoh's Boat* (Houghton Mifflin, 2009) 32p. **IL** 4–9 **RL** 9.5

Imagine you have to complete a 1,000-piece jigsaw puzzle without the picture on the box. You have no idea what the finished puzzle is supposed to look like, and there are thousands of possibilities! Now imagine that those pieces are huge, 4,000-year-old pieces of wood, so fragile that they could break or disintegrate into dust if you touch them the wrong way. Well, in 1954, archaeologists discovered a puzzle like this buried near the Great Pyramid at Giza, Egypt. This is the story of Ahmed Youssef Moustafa, whose job it was to put this puzzle together. It took ten years of painstaking work, but he was finally able to piece the puzzle together and recreate the ancient boat that had been buried with the pharaoh. How did he do it? Read this book to find out!

Ancient Egypt Book List

Most of the books in this list are set in the ancient past. Riordan's series, The Kane Chronicles, is one of the few that includes modern-day characters, but it merits a place on the list because it's new, and I'm predicting that it will make kids want to learn more about ancient Egypt!

Fiction

Adamson, Heather. *Ancient Egypt: An Interactive Adventure* (Capstone, 2009) 112p. **IL** 3–6 **RL** 3.5

This choose-your-own-adventure book takes kids into ancient Egypt.

Moss, Marissa. *The Pharaoh's Secret* (Amulet, 2009) 308p. **IL** 5–8 **RL** 5.3

> While on a trip to modern-day Egypt with their father, ten-year-old Adom and fourteen-year-old Talibah become drawn into a mystery involving an ancient pharaoh.

Riordan, Rick. *The Kane Chronicles: The Red Pyramid* (Hyperion, 2010) 528p. **IL** 4–7 **RL** 4

> Modern-day siblings Sadie and Carter Kane discover that their ancestors were members of an ancient Egyptian order of magicians, and they may need those skills now to fight Set, an evil god from ancient Egypt.

Turner, Ann. *Maia of Thebes, 1463 B.C.* (Scholastic, 2005) 169p. **IL** 4–6

> When thirteen-year-old Maia accuses her uncle of stealing grain from the temple, she is forced to run away to survive.

Nonfiction

Winters, Kay. *Voices of Ancient Egypt.* Illus. Barry Moser (National Geographic, 2003) 32p. **IL** 3–6 **RL** 4.5

> Through first-person poems, this book recreates the voices and illustrates thirteen types of people who lived in ancient Egypt, from the scribe to the herdsman to the embalmer.

Grades 7 and Up—Fiction

Aubin, Henry T. *Rise of the Golden Cobra* (Annick, 2008) 255p. **IL** YA **RL** 4.8

> This fictionalized account of the invasion of ancient Egypt by King Piankhy of Nubia is told through the voice of a fourteen-year-old messenger, Nebi.

Ancient Greece Booktalks

The ancient Greek Empire lasted from around the eighth century B.C.E. until the Romans took over in 146 B.C.E. Why study ancient Greece? For one thing, it is so fun! Stories about the Greek gods are timelessly entertaining, as Percy Jackson fans can attest. The battles of the Trojan War, the voyages of Odysseus, and the foibles and follies of the gods still have appeal. The true stories from ancient Greece are just as fun. The advances they made as a society in architecture, mathematics, science, and philosophy laid the foundation for modern Western thought. And they did it all without computers, iPods, and cell phones—incredible!

Fiction

Cadnum, Michael. *Nightsong: The Legend of Orpheus and Eurydice* (Scholastic, 2006) 133p. **IL** 4–9 **RL** 8.3

This is the story of Prince Orpheus, a singer whose music is a "legend among gods and men." One day Orpheus hears women singing, and when he goes to check it out, he sees Eurydice, the woman with the most beautiful voice, and he falls instantly in love with her. She's a princess and her father is thrilled when they get engaged, but their love is doomed. Eurydice is bitten by a snake and killed on their wedding day. Orpheus practically goes crazy with grief, and in desperation, he decides to attempt the impossible. He goes to the Underworld to try to bring her back. Can he do what no mortal has ever done before?

Cadnum, Michael. *Starfall: Phaeton and the Chariot of the Sun* (Scholastic, 2004) 128p. **IL** 5–9 **RL** 4.5

Phaeton has never met his father, Apollo the sun god, but his mortal mother swears that Phaeton is a demigod, half god, half mortal. Stupid Phaeton makes the mistake of bragging about it though, and no one believes him. If you think about it, it does sound kind of far-fetched. The people think that his mother's story is just a cover-up for a secret affair she doesn't want to admit. So Phaeton gets annoyed and starts to wonder why his father never tried to get in touch with him. Why is his father not here to stick up for him and protect him? He decides to make the journey to the end of the world, to the gates of the sunrise, to confront his father and ask him to prove his love for him. Stupid Phaeton has no idea the consequences he will suffer as a result.

Ellis, Julie. *What's Your Angle Pythagoras? A Math Adventure.* Illus. Phyllis Hornung (Charlesbridge, 2004) 32p. **IL** 3–5 **RL** 3.5

In real life, Pythagoras was the Greek mathematician who discovered the Pythagorean theorem. It's the formula we use to measure the lengths of the sides of a triangle. This picture book imagines what he must have been like when he was young. It's fiction; we don't know anything about the real Pythagoras' childhood, but it's fun to imagine how he would look at the buildings around him in ancient Greece and see how math could help build them better. He noticed that the tower was leaning and wanted to know why. He figured out how to use angles to build straight walls that are evenly perpendicular to the ground—without leaning over. This book goes into some of the math involved, and explains Pythagoras' famous theorem. Even if you're not interested in math, this book is cool because it makes you see how we use it in everyday life. See also *Pythagoras and the Ratios* (Charlesbridge, 2010).

McLaren, Clemence. *Waiting for Odysseus* (Atheneum, 2000) 160p. **IL** 6–9 **RL** 6.2

    Odysseus was a warrior from Ithaca, Greece, who fought in the Trojan War. When he left Ithaca to go fight, his son, Telemachus, was just a baby, but he's been gone for more than eighteen years, and now Telemachus is a grown man trying to protect his mother, Penelope, from the men who want to marry her. She still says that her husband is alive and will come home, but the men all say he's dead and want to force her to take one of them as her new husband. Meanwhile, Odysseus is alive and trying to get home, but he has one problem after another: a fight with a one-eyed giant, a terrible storm that destroyed almost his entire fleet, and being held prisoner by a sorceress who wants him to stay with her. This book tells Odysseus' story through the eyes of his faithful wife Penelope, the sorceress Circe, the goddess Athena, and his childhood nanny Eurycleia. See also *Inside the Walls of Troy* (Simon Pulse, 1996).

Napoli, Donna Jo. *Sirena* (Scholastic, 1998) 210p. **IL** 6–9 **RL** 7.2

    Sirena is a mermaid, and she lives on an island with her mermaid sisters. Their singing is so beautiful that the sailors passing by in ships can't resist their song; they have to steer their ships toward the music. The mermaids want this because the legend says that if a human falls in love with a mermaid, then she will become immortal and live forever. The problem is that the island is surrounded by rocks, and when the sailors steer their ships toward it, they crash on the rocks and drown. Sirena feels so guilty about this that she decides to leave the island and live on her own. But lo and behold, a shipwrecked sailor washes up onto her deserted island, and she nurses him back to health. Of course, he falls in love with her, and she becomes immortal but that's not the end of the story. This is a really good book, but the ending is sad.

◼ Video Booktalk: http://www.bookwink.com/archive_2007_05_22.html

Nonfiction

Mann, Elizabeth. *The Parthenon.* Illus. Yuan Lee (Mikaya, 2006) 48p. **IL** 4–6 **RL** 5.5

    The Parthenon in Athens is one of the most famous and important examples of Greek architecture, but what's so special about it? One of the things that makes it special is its history. It was built as a temple to the goddess Athena, whom Athens is named after, and it was meant to be her home on earth. If you were going to build a house for your god to live in, you would make it pretty special, right? So they built the Parthenon out of the most expensive material they could get: marble. Workers and teams of oxen carried tons of marble eleven miles uphill to the construction site. There, workers cut the stone to super-exact measurements. It had to be perfect because they didn't use any mortar or anything to hold the stones together. They just had to fit together and balance like a huge house of cards. Finally, artists created the sculptures all along the outside. But the most spectacular sculpture was the forty-foot statue of Athena covered entirely with gold and ivory—2,500 pounds of gold! The statue is destroyed now, and the Parthenon is just a skeleton of rock remains, but this book makes it easy to see why it is so famous. It makes me wish I could have seen it in real life in all its glory.

Reynolds, Susan. *The First Marathon: The Legend of Pheidippides.* Illus. Daniel Minter (Albert Whitman & Company, 2006) 32p. **IL** 3–5 **RL** 5

    Today we call a 26-mile running race a marathon, but how did it get that name? This is the fascinating story of Pheidippides, who ran 280 miles in one week to help Athens in the battle against the invading Persians. Where did the battle take place? In a Greek town called Marathon. After all that running, Pheiddipides still had to fight in the battle, and when it was over, he had to complete one more task: an almost 26-mile run from Marathon to Athens to tell the people about the battle. If you have ever seen people running a marathon, you know that after 26 miles, they look pretty tired. Imagine how tired you would be at the end of the week if you had run 280 miles! Read this picture book to find out what happened at the battle, what happened to Pheidippides, and how the modern-day marathon came about.

Trumble, Kelly. *The Library of Alexandria.* Illus. Robina MacIntyre Marshall (Clarion, 2003) 72p. **IL** 5–9 **RL** 7

    Technically, the library of Alexandria is in Egypt, but when it was built, it was a part of the great Greek Empire. It was the best library of its time and shows how important scholarship was to the ancient Greeks. They made some incredible scientific and mathematical discoveries. For example, Eratosthenes discovered a way to use geometry to calculate the distance around the entire earth. Yes, the ancient Greeks knew that the earth wasn't flat! The library and all its books were destroyed during Cleopatra's reign when the Romans conquered most of the Greek Empire. At that time, every book was hand copied, so some of these books were the only copies in the world. If those books had survived, maybe the people in Columbus' day, hundreds of years later, would have been able to read Eratosthenes and know that the earth was round.

Ancient Greece Book List

Fans of Rick Riordan's <u>Percy Jackson</u> series will find plenty more books in this list to get excited about. Although Percy is a modern-day character, these books are all set in ancient times and will really make kids feel like they are there.

Fiction

Caper, William. *Ancient Greece: An Interactive History Adventure* (Capstone, 2010) 112p. **IL** 3–6 **RL** 3.5

The second-person narrative allows the reader to choose different story paths in this choose-your-own-adventure book set in ancient Greece.

Friesner, Esther. *Nobody's Princess* (Random House, 2007) 305p. **IL** 5–9 **RL** 5.9

This story imagines the girlhood of the beautiful Helen, the girl who will go on to become queen of Sparta, and later Helen of Troy, but for now she is a tomboy eager to fight and have adventures. See also the sequel *Nobody's Prize* (Random House, 2008).

Karas, G. Brian. *Young Zeus* (Scholastic, 2010) 48p. **IL** 1–4 **RL** 2.3

This humorous picture book imagines Zeus as a young boy and teenager.

Kindl, Patrice. *Lost in the Labyrinth* (Houghton Mifflin, 2002) 194p. **IL** 5–9 **RL** 6

Princess Xenodice tries to protect her half-brother, the Minotaur, from those who think he is a soulless monster and want to have him killed.

Landmann, Bimba. *The Incredible Voyage of Ulysses* (Getty, 2010) 60p. **IL** 5–8

A graphic novel version of *The Odyssey.*

McCaughrean, Geraldine. *Odysseus* (Cricket, 2004) 128p. **IL** 4–9 **RL** 6

This collection features the adventures of Odysseus, including his encounters with the evil Cyclops, the monsters Scylla and Charybdis, the beautiful sorceress Circe, and the vengeful god of the sea, Poseidon.

McLaren, Clemence. *Aphrodite's Blessings* (Atheneum, 2002) 202p. **IL** 6–9 **RL** 6.5

Atalanta, Andromeda, and Psyche, three female characters in Greek mythology tell the stories of their marriages.

O'Connor, George. *Zeus: King of the Gods* (First Second, 2010) 80p. **IL** 4–9 **RL** 4.7

The first in a new graphic novel series, this book tells the complete story of Zeus. See also *Athena: Grey-Eyed Goddess* (First Second, 2010).

Scieszka, Jon. *It's All Greek to Me.* Illus. Lane Smith (Viking, 1999) 73p. **IL** 3–6 **RL** 4.1

Three modern-day boys are transported back to the time of Zeus and the other gods in Greek mythology.

Nonfiction

Love, D. Anne. *Of Numbers and Stars: The Story of Hypatia.* Illus. Pam Paparone (Holiday House, 2006) 32p. **IL** 2–5 **RL** 7.4

In the fourth century C.E., Greek women were not typically educated, but Hypatia's father taught her mathematics, astronomy, and philosophy, and she became a well-known scholar and teacher. This picture book biography depicts her unique life among the scholars of Alexandria.

Grades 7 and Up—Fiction

Cooney, Caroline B. *Goddess of Yesterday* (Delacorte, 2002) 264p. **IL** YA **RL** 6.1

> Anaxandra lives in the castle with King Menelaus and his wife Helen, until the Trojan prince, Paris, comes and has an affair with Helen, leading to the Trojan War.

Geras, Adele. *Troy* (Harcourt, 2001) 352p. **IL** YA **RL** 7.1

> The women of Troy describe the gruesome battles and dangerous love affairs that were broiling during the last weeks of the Trojan War. See also *Ithaka* (Harcourt, 2007).

Halam, Ann. *Snakehead* (Wendy Lamb, 2008) 287p. **IL** YA **RL** 3.7

> Demigod Perseus, son of Zeus and a human mother, falls in love with Andromeda, a mysterious princess trying to escape her tragic fate.

Spinner, Stephanie. *Quiver* (Random House, 2002) 177p. **IL** YA **RL** 5.7

> Atalanta's father abandoned her when she was a baby, but she was rescued and raised by hunters in the forest. Now her father, King Oeneus, needs an heir and commands that she come back, marry, and take her rightful place in the castle. Atalanta does not want to, but does she have a choice? See also *Quicksilver* (Random House, 2005).

Ancient Rome Booktalks

The ancient Roman Empire started in Rome, Italy, in the eighth century B.C.E. and spread throughout Europe over the next 1,200 years, conquering everything in its path. Many twenty-first-century readers, especially females, may not find much to admire about the ancient Romans. The predominant themes running through these books are slavery, brutal gladiator fights, machine-like military strength, and the apocalyptic volcanic destruction of Pompeii. So it should be no problem getting boys excited about them!

Fiction

Banks, Lynn Reid. *Tiger, Tiger* (Random House, 2004) 195p. **IL** 5–8 **RL** 5.4

In ancient Rome, it was common to capture exotic wild animals from all over the world to bring them back and display them in the Roman "circus." But this circus was nothing like any circus you could see today. In the Roman circus, the animals would be sent out into the arena with condemned criminals, and they would fight to the death, or sometimes the animals would just devour the humans without a fight. This was the Roman idea of entertainment. Pretty sick, huh? As this book starts, Roman hunters are capturing two brother tiger cubs. The tigers are terrified and miserable as they are taken away from their mother and put in a cage in the bottom of the ship to Rome. When they arrive, they are each sent to live very different lives. The bigger tiger, Brute, is taken to the arena to be trained as a killer. It is a horrible life of abuse and hunger and ferocious anger at his human handlers. The smaller tiger, Boots, is sent to become the tame pet of Emperor Caesar's daughter, Aurelia. Aurelia loves her new pet, and Boots lives a pampered life of affection, safety, and plenty of food. After a while, Boots and Brute begin to forget about each other as they get used to their new lives, but then, when they least expect it, they meet again in the most shocking of circumstances.

Denenberg, Barry. *Atticus of Rome, 30 B.C.* (Scholastic, 2004) 166p. **IL** 4–8 **RL** 8.6

When Atticus is twelve years old, Roman soldiers invade his village and destroy everything, taking all the survivors as prisoners. Atticus and father survive and are taken to Rome and sold in the slave market. They are separated, and Atticus doesn't know whether he will ever see his father again. But Atticus is lucky. He is bought by Lucius, a rich senator. As a senator, Lucius is a very important man in Roman society, but what really matters to Atticus is that Lucius is a kind and good man who treats him well. Atticus comes to really respect him, so when Lucius entrusts him with an important task, Atticus tries his best to do a good job. Lucius suspects that there is a plot against the emperor, and he asks Atticus to do some spying to see what he can find out. He is sent to follow a wealthy and powerful man named Galerius—but not be seen, of course—and to report everyone whom Galerius meets. Atticus does this, but he is shocked when one of the people Galerius meets is Lucius' own wife. Is she involved in the plot against the emperor? The mystery part of this book is good, but the description of the gladiator fight after the mystery is solved is especially interesting. You'll really feel like you're there, and there is a surprise twist at the end.

Lawrence, Caroline. *The Thieves of Ostia* (Roaring Brook, 2001) 152p. ▊ 4–7 **RL** 5.3

The year is 79 C.E., and Flavia is a free Roman girl living in Ostia with her father. It is her birthday, and she wants to buy a scroll (a book) of her favorite story, *The Aeneid*. But she changes her mind when she goes to the market and sees a group of people being sold as slaves. She decides instead to buy one of the slaves, a girl her age named Nubia, so she can give her a better life. So she and Nubia become friends, and they also become friends with a new neighbor, Jonathan, when he saves Flavia from a pack of wild dogs. It was a really scary experience, but not nearly as scary as what happened later to Jonathan's dog. One day they came home and found that someone had broken into the house and beheaded the dog. One of the neighbors saw a man running away with a bag that looked like it might have the head in it. Flavia loves to solve mysteries, and she wants to get to the bottom of this, but there are dangerous characters around, and what kind of crazy person cuts off a dog's head? This book is perfect for mystery lovers and anyone interested in how people lived in ancient Rome. See also the other books in the Roman Mysteries series.

Platt, Richard. *Roman Diary: The Journal of Iliona of Mytilini, Who Was Captured and Sold as a Slave in Rome, AD 107.* Illus. David Parkins (Candlewick, 2009) 64p. ▊ 4–6 **RL** 6

Iliona is thrilled to be sailing with her family from Greece to Alexandria in Egypt. They will be living there for two years at least while her father rebuilds one of his warehouses that burned down. It will be a huge new adventure for her, so she starts a diary to record everything that happens. But on their fifth day at sea, pirates attack the ship and kill both her parents. Iliona and her younger brother are taken as slaves to be sold in the Roman market. Thankfully, the same master buys them both so they won't be separated, but their lives as Roman slaves are very different from their former lives as wealthy Greeks. Iliona keeps writing in her diary about her new life in Rome. At first she thought she would be chained up and beaten as a slave, but her master is kind, and she is treated very well. She takes care of the master's baby, Lydia, and after a while, Lydia feels like her own little sister. But Iliona's brother has a much more difficult life as a farm worker on the master's country estate, so Iliona saves every coin she can get to buy his freedom. Slaves are really expensive, though, and Iliona does not actually get very many coins. It will take years and years, maybe even a lifetime, to save enough money. Will she and her brother be slaves their whole lives, or is there anything else she can do to win their freedom? Read this book to find out.

Nonfiction

Bingham, Jane. *Look Around a Roman Amphitheater* (Arcturus, 2008) 32p. **IL** 4–7 **RL** 6

This book describes "the Games" that the Romans would go to see for fun. You know how we like go see soccer games or baseball games? Well, the ancient Romans' idea of fun was a lot more brutal! First came the wild animals. But these were not tame little circus acts. These animals would either be hunted and killed or they would fight each other to the death. Either way, a lot of blood was involved. Then there would be public executions in which criminals who were condemned to death would be killed in various horrible ways: torn apart by lions, burned at the stake, or crucified on wooden crosses. Finally would come the highlight of the day, the gladiator fights. Two warriors would fight each other using whatever weapons were assigned to them for that day. If the gladiator won the fight, he could earn money, glory, and fame, but if he lost, he could be killed. It's up to the audience to decide whether the winner gets to kill the loser. Yikes! After reading this book, you may be really glad you were not alive in ancient Roman times!

Blacklock, David. *The Roman Army.* Illus. David Kennet (Walker, 2004) 48p. **IL** 5–8 **RL** 7.8

The Roman Empire lasted from 27 B.C.E. until 476 C.E., and during that time, the Roman army was an unstoppable power, conquering territory and enforcing Roman law. How did they manage to keep control over such a huge part of the world for so long? They were massive, sure, but the brilliance of the Roman army goes beyond just the number of its troops. This book describes the military training, the weapons, the battle formation, and strategy that made the Roman army such a fearsome force. If you are interested in war history and the military, you will be fascinated by this book.

Deem, James M. *Bodies from the Ash: Life and Death in Ancient Pompeii* (Houghton Mifflin, 2005) 48p. **IL** 4–8 **RL** 6.2

On Tuesday August 24, 79 C.E., Mount Vesuvius began to erupt. Within twenty-four hours, the entire city of Pompeii had been utterly annihilated. Every human, plant, and animal that found itself in the city on that day was either burned or buried alive in the explosion. This book gives an hour-by-hour account of what that day was probably like for the citizens of Pompeii before they died. It describes each stage of the eruption from the first stage of rocks falling from sky like rain, to the second stage of 600-degree lava flowing at speeds of up to 180 miles per hour, to the final and deadliest stage, when all the remaining rocks and debris that had been hovering above in a volcanic cloud, just collapsed onto the people of Pompeii, destroying everything and burying them in twelve feet of ash. Over the years, people forgot about this city. There were no records and probably few survivors who escaped. It was as if Pompeii had never existed. But hundreds of years later, archaeological excavations began to unearth all the bodies that had been buried under layers of volcanic rubble. The most exciting thing they found was that the shape of the people's bodies had been preserved in the ash. Not the bodies themselves, but kind of mummified casts of their bodies, so anyone could see what their last moments on earth were like. This is a really interesting book about history even if you're not into dead bodies, but be warned: some of the pictures are a little gruesome.

Mack, Lorrie. *Ancient Rome* (Dorling Kindersley, 2009) 48p. **IL** 4–8

During the time of the Roman Empire, Rome had more wealth and power than any nation anywhere, ever. It had the strongest army and literally ruled the world. This book shows you the map and describes the battles fought by the Roman army. It also describes what life was like for ordinary Romans. They had a senate just like us, but instead of an elected president, they had an emperor. One emperor was so vicious, he was named Septimus Severus. *Severus* means "cruel" in Latin. Do you think that's where Severus Snape got his name? They had sports and entertainment just like us, but their games involved weapons and man-eating animals. Obviously they were a lot bloodier than our Superbowl! They had elaborate dinners with bread and cheese and meat, but they also ate some unusual things (peacock brains anyone?) and some downright disgusting things like a sauce made from rotted fish guts. This book really makes you imagine what your life would be like if you were living back then.

Ancient Rome Book List

Obviously, boys will love the books in this list, but several of them do attempt to show Roman life from a female perspective. Girls can read them and see themselves in the human emotions of the characters, their families, friendships, and loves . . . and be really, really glad that they didn't live back then!

Fiction

Hanel, Rachael. *Ancient Rome: An Interactive History* (Capstone, 2010) 112p. **IL** 3–6 **RL** 3.5

A choose-your-own-adventure story about life in ancient Rome.

Moss, Marissa. *Galen: My Life in Imperial Rome* (Harcourt, 2002) 48p. **IL** 3–6 **RL** 5

This illustrated diary of a fictional slave in Rome shows what life was like then.

Price, Robin. *I Am Spartapuss* (Mogzilla, 2004) 190p. **IL** 3–5

Set in Rome 36 C.E., when the mighty Feline Empire ruled the world, Spartapuss must survive gladiator training school and brave the perils of the Arena. See also the other books in the Spartapuss Tales series.

Scieszka, Jon. *See You Later, Gladiator.* Illus. Adam McCauley (Viking, 2000) 87p. **IL** 3–6 **RL** 4.3

Three modern-day kids travel back in time to ancient Rome where they rely on pro wrestling moves when forced to fight as gladiators in the Coliseum.

Nonfiction

Chandler, Fiona, Sam Taplin, and Jane Bingham. *The Usborne Encyclopedia of the Roman World* (Scholastic, 2001) 128p. **IL** 4–7

Everything you ever wanted to know about the Roman Empire is explained and illustrated in this brief encyclopedia.

Osborne, Mary Pope. *Pompeii: Lost and Found.* Illus. Bonnie Christensen (Knopf, 2006) 32p. **IL** 3–5 **RL** 4.5

This book uses frescoes to illustrate what daily life was like in Pompeii in the year 79 C.E. before the volcano eruption that buried the city for 1700 years.

Sonneborn, Liz. *The Romans: Life in Ancient Rome.* Illus. Samuel Hiti (Millbrook, 2010) 48p. **IL** 4–7 **RL** 3.4

Photos and comic book drawings show everyday life in ancient Rome, including religion, inventions, building, and government.

Grades 7 and Up—Fiction

Harris, Robert. *Pompeii* (Random House, 2003) 368p. **IL** YA **RL** 6

The Roman Empire's richest citizens are relaxing without a care, but their world is about to be destroyed, and only one man is worried. The young engineer Marcus Attilius Primus has just taken charge of the Aqua Augusta, the aqueduct that brings fresh water to a quarter of a million people in nine towns around the Bay of Naples. Springs are failing for the first time in generations, but by the time Marcus discovers why, it is too late.

Lasky, Kathryn. *The Last Girls of Pompeii* (Viking, 2007) 184p. **IL** YA **RL** 4.5

Julia and her slave girl are best friends even though their futures hold very different paths, but none of that matters anymore when Mt. Vesuvius erupts.

McKeown, Adam. *The Young Reader's Shakespeare: Julius Caesar.* Illus. Janet Hamlin (Sterling, 2008) 80p. **IL** YA **RL** 4

A retelling of the famous Shakespeare play in which a group of senators murder General Caesar before he crowns himself king and ends democracy in Rome.

Index